CW00428381

ANNOUNCING THE HAVE:
NOW IN PREPARATION FOR P

The edition of *The Complete Works of Frances Rid*

Volume I *Behold Your King:*
The Complete Poetical Works of Frances Ridley Havergal

Volume II *Whose I Am and Whom I Serve:*
Prose Works of Frances Ridley Havergal

Volume III *Loving Messages for the Little Ones:*
Works for Children by Frances Ridley Havergal

Volume IV *Love for Love: Frances Ridley Havergal:*
Memorials, Letters and Biographical Works

Volume V *Songs of Truth and Love:*
Music by Frances Ridley Havergal and William Henry Havergal

David L. Chalkley, Editor   Dr. Glen T. Wegge, Music Editor

The Music of Frances Ridley Havergal by Glen T. Wegge, Ph.D.

This Companion Volume to the Havergal edition is a valuable presentation of F.R.H.'s extant scores. Except for a very few of her hymntunes published in hymnbooks, most or nearly all of F.R.H.'s scores have been very little—if any at all—seen, or even known of, for nearly a century. What a valuable body of music has been unknown for so long and is now made available to many. Dr. Wegge completed his Ph.D. in Music Theory at Indiana University at Bloomington, and his diligence and thoroughness in this volume are obvious. First an analysis of F.R.H.'s compositions is given, an essay that both addresses the most advanced musicians and also reaches those who are untrained in music; then all the extant scores that have been found are newly typeset, with complete texts for each score and extensive indices at the end of the book. This volume presents F.R.H.'s music in newly typeset scores diligently prepared by Dr. Wegge, and Volume V of the Havergal edition presents the scores in facsimile, the original 19th century scores. (The essay—a dissertation—analysing her scores is given the same both in this Companion Volume and in Volume V of the Havergal edition.)

Dr. Wegge is also preparing all of these scores for publication in performance folio editions.

Frances Ridley Havergal, portrait in chalk, drawn by T. J. Hughes in February, 1879. Her sister Maria recommended this portrait as so life-like. Below this is a notice printed in the newspaper The Christian *for July 3, 1879, one month after F.R.H. died on June 3.*

THE LATE MISS F. RIDLEY HAVERGAL.—Mr. T. J. Hughes, of 2, Elm-row, Hampstead, has shown us a portrait in chalk for which Miss Havergal sat to him several times. This likeness is recommended by her sister, Miss M. V. G. Havergal, as being so life-like. Orders for photographic copies, at a guinea each, may be sent to Mr. Hughes.

Red Letter Days

A REGISTER OF

Anniversaries and Birthdays

BY

FRANCES RIDLEY HAVERGAL

"Knowing her intense desire that Christ should be magnified, whether
by her life or in her death, may it be to His glory
that in these pages she, being dead,
'Yet speaketh ! ' "

Taken from the Edition of *The Complete Works of Frances Ridley Havergal.*

David L. Chalkley, Editor   Dr. Glen T. Wegge, Associate Editor

ISBN 978-1-937236-18-2   Library of Congress: 2011919007

Book cover by Sherry Goodwin and David Carter.

PREFACE.

W E read in Bible story of the Jews having "joy and gladness, a feast, and a good day;" and according to the wise old ways of the times, when there were fewer books and less history, they "ordained that these days should be remembered and kept throughout every family."

What a splendid record of sunny days most of us would have had by this time, if we had kept account of them all along! It may be true enough that "into each life some rain must fall;" but it is no less true that upon each life some sunbeams fall. Why should we not gather them up, and keep a book of remembrance for all the pleasant and happy times, and all the "good days" that God gives us? If we systematically did this, what light "His love in time past" would throw upon time present!

Too often we are more ready to note the anniversary of a sorrow than of a joy, unless the latter happens to be the conventionally observed "birthday." Let us try a fresh plan, and keep a record of our red letter days; for when a day of any special "light and gladness" comes (Esther 8:16), whatever may be the occurrence which makes it such to us, we may well call it a red letter day—that is, a day of holy festival, and thenceforth of hallowed remembrance. I think many of us will be astonished in a very few years to find how many such days we have to be thankful for, if we honestly record them, and what an altogether brighter view of life a glance through this little book will give them; and, better still, it will stimulate our faith, our hope, our love, and, most of all, our gratitude for the goodness and mercy which surely follow us *all* the days of our lives, even the dark ones.

The verses for each day in this little book have been selected at the request of the Publishers, and this is my only apology for them. It is a pleasure to offer my readers the more valuable addition of verses by my sainted father for each month in the year.

FRANCES RIDLEY HAVERGAL

May, 1879.

MEMORIAL NAMES.

––––––––

THE High Priest stands before the mercy-seat,

    And on his breast bright mingling jewel-flames

    Reflect Shechinah light; twelve patriarch names

Flash where the emerald and sapphire meet

Sardius and diamond. With softer beam,

    From mystic onyx on his shoulders placed,

    Deep graven, never altered or erased,

The same great names, *in birthday order,* gleam.

May each name written here be thus engraved,

    Set in the place of power, the place of love,

    And borne in sweet memorial above.

By Him who loved and chose, redeemed and saved.

Be each dear name, the greatest and the least,

Always upon the heart of our High Priest.

                          —*Frances Ridley Havergal*

OUR RED LETTER DAYS.

———

My Alpine staff recalls each shining height,

    Each pass of grandeur with rejoicing gained,

    Carved with a lengthening record, self-explained,

Of mountain-memories sublime and bright.

No valley-life but hath some mountain days,

    Bright summits in the retrospective view,

    And toil-won passes to glad prospects new,

Fair sunlit memories of joy and praise.

Here then inscribe them,—each "red letter day!"

Forget not all the sunshine of the way

By which the Lord hath led thee; answered prayers

And joys unasked, strange blessings, lifted cares,

Grand promise-echoes! Thus each page shall be

A record of God's love and faithfulness to thee!

—*Frances Ridley Havergal*

JANUARY.

BY REV. WILLIAM HENRY HAVERGAL, M.A.,
Hon. Canon of Worcester Cathedral.

"My times are in Thy hand,"
　　Their best and fittest place;
I would not have them at command
　　Without Thy guiding grace.

"My times," and yet not mine;
　　I cannot them ordain;
Not one e'er waits from me a sign,
　　Nor can I one detain.

"My times," O Lord, are Thine,
　　And Thine their oversight:
Thy wisdom, love, and power combine
　　To make them dark or bright.

I know not what shall be,
　　When passing times are fled;
But all events I leave with Thee,
　　And calmly bow my head.

Hence, Lord, in Thee I rest,
　　And wait Thy holy will;
I lean upon my Saviour's breast,
　　Or gladly go on still.

And when my "times" shall cease,
　　And life shall fade away,
Then bid me, Lord, depart in peace
　　To realms of endless day!

W. H. H.

January 1.

Circumcision.

Mᴚ soul thirsteth for Thee.—Psalm 63:1.
He satisfieth the longing soul.—Psalm 107:9.
I will come to you.—John 14:18.

"Certainly I will be with thee!" Let me feel it, Saviour dear,
Let me know that Thou art with me, very precious, very near.
On this day of solemn pausing, with Thyself all longing still.
Let Thy pardon, let Thy presence, let Thy peace my spirit fill.

January 2.

Wʜᴏ hitherto waited in the king's gate.—1 Chronicles 9:18.
Leaning upon her Beloved.—Song of Solomon 8:5.

Another year is dawning!
Dear Master, let it be
In working or in waiting.
Another year with Thee.
Another year of leaning
Upon Thy loving breast,
Of ever-deepening trustfulness,
Of quiet, happy rest.

January 3.

Bᴇʜᴏʟᴅ, I am with thee, and will keep thee in all places whither thou
goest; for I will not leave thee, until I have done that which I have
spoken to thee of.—Genesis 28:15.

Another year of progress, another year of praise,
Another year of proving Thy presence all the days.
Another year of service, of witness for Thy love.
Another year of training for holier work above.

January 4.

Mᴚ Spirit remaineth among you: fear ye not.—Haggai 2:5.
The anointing which ye have received of Him abideth in you.
—1 John 2:27.

"Certainly I will be with thee!" Blessed Spirit, come to me,
Rest upon me, dwell within me, let my heart Thy temple be;
Through the trackless year before me, Holy One, with me abide!
Teach me, comfort me, and calm me, be my ever-present Guide.

January 5.

I PRESS toward the mark.—Philippians 3:14.
From strength to strength.—Psalm 84:7.
From glory to glory.—2 Corinthians 3:18.

Now onward, ever onward, "from strength to strength" we go,
While "grace for grace" abundantly shall from His fulness flow,
To glory's full fruition, from glory's foretaste here,
Until His Very Presence crown our happiest New Year!

January 6.

Epiphany.

I HAVE manifested Thy name unto the men which Thou gavest Me out
of the world.—John 17:6.

He came to tell the Father's love,
His wisdom, truth, and grace;
To show the brightness of His smile,
The glory of His face:
With His own light, so full and bright,
The shades of death to chase.

January 7.

AND when they had opened their treasures, they presented unto Him
gifts; gold, and frankincense, and myrrh.—Matthew 2:11.

Take my love; my Lord, I pour
At thy feet its treasure store.
Take myself, and I will be
Ever, *only*, ALL for Thee!

January 8.

THOU hast avouched the Lord this day to be thy God.—Deuteronomy 26:17.

For thou hast confirmed to Thyself Thy people Israel to be a people unto Thee for ever.—2 Samuel 7:24.

> In full and glad surrender, I give myself to Thee;
> Thine utterly, and only, and evermore to be!
>
> O Son of God, who lovest me, I will be Thine alone;
> And all I am, and all I have, shall henceforth be Thine own!

January 9.

MY God shall supply all your need according to His riches in glory by Christ Jesus.—Philippians 4:19.

Always having all sufficiency in all things.—2 Corinthians 9:8.

> For the year before us, O what rich supplies!
> For the poor and needy, living streams shall rise:
> For the sad and sinful shall His grace abound,
> For the faint and feeble perfect strength be found.

January 10.

I SAID, I will never break My covenant with you.—Judges 2:1.

There failed not ought of any good thing which the Lord had spoken unto the house of Israel.—Joshua 21:45.

> He will never fail us, He will not forsake;
> His eternal covenant He will never break.
> Resting on His promise, what have we to fear?
> God is all-sufficient for the coming year!

January 11.

NOW the God of hope fill you with all joy and peace in believing, that ye may abound in hope, through the power of the Holy Ghost. —Romans 15:13.

> Faith that increaseth,
> Walking in light;
> Hope that aboundeth,
> Glowing and bright;

Love that is perfect,
Casting out fear,
Crown with rejoicing
Thine opening year.

January 12.

Ye are Christ's.—1 Corinthians 3:23.

Christ hath called thee, Christ hath blessed!
Everlasting life is thine;
Closely cleaving, thou shalt rest
In His changeless love divine.
Let Him teach thee what He will,
In thee day by day fulfil
All His sweet and blessèd will.

January 13.

Blessed be the God and Father of our Lord Jesus Christ, who hath blessed us with all spiritual blessings in heavenly places in Christ.
—Ephesians 1:3.

Blessings unspoken this year be thine!
Each day in its rainbow flight entwine
New gems in thy joy-wreathed crown!
May each in the smile of Him be bright,
Who is Changeless Love and Eternal Light,
Till the glory seem to thy trancèd sight
As heaven to earth come down.

January 14.

In the light of the King's countenance is life.—Proverbs 16:15.
The Lord lift up His countenance upon thee, and give thee peace.
—Numbers 6:26.

Peace in the Saviour, rest at His feet;
Smile of His countenance, radiant and sweet.
Joy in His Presence, Christ ever near!
Such be thy treasure all through the year.

January 15.

WE rest on Thee.—2 Chronicles 14:11.

Resting on the faithfulness of Christ our Lord,
Resting on the fulness of His own sure word,
Resting on His power, on His love untold,
Resting on His covenant secured of old.

January 16.

THESE things have I spoken unto you, that in Me ye might have peace.
—John 16:33.

There is a point of rest
At the great centre of the cyclone's force,
A silence at its secret source;
A little child might slumber undistressed,
Without the ruffle of one fairy curl,
In that strange central calm amid the mighty whirl.

January 17.

WHAT He hath prepared for him that waiteth for Him.—Isaiah 64:4.

Not death, but life; not silence, but the strings
Of angel-harps; no deep cold sea, but springs
Of living water; no dim, wearied sight,
Nor time, nor tear-mist, but the joy of light;
Not sleep, but rest, that happy service brings.

January 18.

THOU hast made him most blessed for ever.—Psalm 21:6.

The music of his life
Is nowise stilled, but blended so with songs
Around the throne of God, that our poor ears
No longer hear it.

January 19.

PRAISE waiteth for Thee.—Psalm 65:1.

The sweetest music here
Calls forth the quiet tear,
For grief and gladness flow in blended stream ;
Oh for the joyous day,
(Can it be far away?)
When one great alleluia-song shall chase
Life's tuneless dream!

January 20.

SURELY goodness and mercy shall follow me all the days of my life.
—Psalm 23:6.

When thy days are veiled in night,
Christ shall give thee heavenly light;
Seem they wearisome and long,
Yet in Him thou shalt be strong.
Cold and wintry though they prove,
Thine the sunshine of His love;
Or, with fervid heat oppressed,
In His shadow thou shalt rest.

January 21.

YE are not your own. For ye are bought with a price: therefore
glorify God in your body, and in your spirit, which are God's.
—1 Corinthians 6:19, 20.

"Not your own!" To Him ye owe
All your life and all your love.
Live that ye His praise may show,
Who is yet all praise above.
Every day and every hour,
Every gift and every power,
Consecrate to Him alone,
Who hath claimed you for His own.

——— *January 22.* ———

Tʜᴇ Lord taketh pleasure in them that fear Him, in those that hope in His mercy.—Psalm 147:11.

> O mystery of grace,
> That chooseth us to stand before Thy face;
> To be Thy "special treasure,"
> Thy portion, Thy delight, Thine own;
> That taketh pleasure
> In them that fear Thy name, that hope alone
> In Thy sweet mercy's boundless measure.

——— *January 23.* ———

Lᴇᴀᴠᴇ me not, neither forsake me, O God of my salvation.—Psalm 27:9. He hath said, I will never leave thee, nor forsake thee.—Hebrews 13:5.

> He is with thee! thine own Master,
> Leading, loving to the end!
> Brightening joy and lightening sorrow,
> *All* to-day, yet more to-morrow,
> King and Saviour, Lord and Friend.

——— *January 24.* ———

I ʟᴏᴠᴇ my Master, . . . I will not go out free.—Exodus 21:5.

> My Master shed His life-blood
> My vassal-life to win,
> And save me from the bondage
> Of tyrant self and sin.
> Rejoicing and adoring,
> Henceforth my song shall be,
> I love, I love my Master,
> I will not go out free!

——— *January 25.* ———

Conversion of St. Paul.

Wʜᴏsᴇ I am, and whom I serve.—Acts 27:23.

Jesus, Master! I am Thine;
　Keep me faithful, keep me near;
Let Thy presence in me shine,
　All my onward way to cheer.
Jesus! at Thy feet I fall;
　Oh, be Thou my All in all.

January 26.

For Thy sake.—John 13:37.
　Keep this for ever in the imagination of the thoughts of the heart of Thy people.—1 Chronicles 29:18.

Only for Jesus! Lord, keep it for ever,
　Sealed on the heart and engraved on the life!
Pulse of all gladness and nerve of endeavour,
　Secret of rest, and the strength of our strife.

January 27.

Underneath are the everlasting arms.—Deuteronomy 33:27.
　I will uphold thee with the right hand of My righteousness.
—Isaiah 41:10.

I am so weak, dear Lord! I cannot stand
　One moment without Thee;
But oh! the tenderness of Thine enfolding,
And oh! the faithfulness of Thine upholding,
And oh! the strength of Thy right hand!
　That strength is enough for me.

January 28.

Be strong in the Lord, and in the power of His might. Above all, taking the shield of faith, wherewith ye shall be able to quench all the fiery darts of the wicked.—Ephesians 6:10, 16.

Distrust thyself, but trust His strength;
　In Him thou shalt be strong!
His weakest ones may learn at length
　A daily triumph-song.

—————————— *January 29.* ——————————

CANST thou find out the Almighty unto perfection?—Job 11:7.

> Unseen things
> Remain unfathomed and unsounded,
> And hidden as the springs
> Of an immeasurable sea,
> Because His thought, sublime and great,
> No language finds commensurate
> With its infinity.

—————————— *January 30.* ——————————

WHAT is that to thee? Follow thou Me.—John 21:22.

> What though to-day
> Thou canst not trace at all the hidden reason
> For His strange dealings through the trial-season,
> Trust and obey!
> Though God's cloud-mystery enfold thee here,
> In after life and light all shall be plain and clear.

—————————— *January 31.* ——————————

HE doeth according to His will.—Daniel 4:35.
Do Thou for me.—Psalm 109:21.

In Thy sovereignty rejoicing, we Thy children vow and praise,
For we know that kind and loving, just and true are all Thy ways,
While Thy heart of sovereign mercy, and Thine arm of sovereign might,
For our great and strong salvation in Thy sovereign grace unite.

FEBRUARY.

Shout, O earth! from silence waking,
    Tune with joy thy varied tongue:
Shout! as when, from chaos breaking,
    Sweetly flowed the natal song.
Shout! for thy Creator's love
Sends redemption from above.

Downward, from His star-paved dwelling,
    Comes the incarnate Son of God:
Countless voices thrilling, swelling,
    Tell the triumphs of His blood.
Shout! He comes thy tribes to bless
With His spotless righteousness.

Call Him blessèd! on thy mountains,
    In thy wilds, and citied plains:
Call Him blessèd! where thy fountains
    Speak in softly murmuring strains.
Let thy captives, let thy kings,
Join the lyre of thousand strings.

Blessèd Lord, and Lord of blessing!
    Pour Thy quickening gifts abroad;
Raptured tongues, Thy love confessing,
    Shall extol the living God.
Blessèd, Blessèd, Blessèd Lord!
Heaven shall chant no other word!

W. H. H.

——————— *February 1.* ———————

G OD commendeth His love towards us, in that, while we were yet sinners, Christ died for us.—Romans 5:8.

The meeting blest
Of His great love and foreseen human woe,
Struck forth a mighty fire that sent a glow
Throughout the universe, lit gloriously
The farthest vistas of eternity,
And, flooding heaven itself with radiance new,
Revealed the heart of God, all-merciful, all-true.

——————— *February 2.* ———————

Purification of the Virgin Mary.

H AVING therefore, brethren, boldness to enter into the holiest by the blood of Jesus. . ..Let us draw near with a true heart in full assurance of faith, having our hearts sprinkled.—Hebrews 10:19, 22.

Now the holiest with boldness
We may enter in,
For the open fountain cleanseth
From all sin!

——————— *February 3.* ———————

A ND to know the love of Christ, which passeth knowledge, that ye might be filled with all the fulness of God.—Ephesians 3:19.

Take us, Lord, O take us truly,
Mind and soul and heart and will;
Empty us and cleanse us throughly,
Then with all Thy fulness fill.
Lord, we ask it, hardly knowing
What this wondrous gift may be,
But fulfil to overflowing,
Thy great meaning let us see.

——————— *February 4.* ———————

B ELOVED, let us love one another: for love is of God.—1 John 4:7.

Perhaps the heart you meet so coldly
Burns with deepest lava-glow;
Wisely pierce the crust, and boldly,
And a fervid stream shall flow.
Dialects of love are many,
Though the language be but one;
Study all you can, or any,
While life's precious school-hours run.

February 5.

CONTINUE ye in My love. Love one another, as I have loved you.
—John 15:9, 12.

Yes, loving each other, blessing and blessed
In the strength of our gladness, calm and bright;
But with more of blessing and love for all
The smile shall beam and the song shall fall,
Touching the shadows round with light;
Because in His love we are nevermore lonely,
Because we will live for Him ever and only.

February 6.

LOVE is of God.—1 John 4:7.

It is a blessèd gift,
Not shared by all alike—the power to love;
And not less blessèd for proportioned pain,
Its fiery seal, its royal crown of thorns.

February 7.

WHO comforteth us in all our tribulation, that we may be able to
comfort them which are in any trouble, by the comfort wherewith
we ourselves are comforted of God.—2 Corinthians 1:4.

Seldom can the heart be lonely
If it seek a lonelier still,
Self-forgetting, seeking only
Emptier cups of love to fill.

— *February 8.* —

WHETHER we be afflicted, it is for your consolation and salvation: or whether we be comforted, it is for your consolation and salvation.
—2 Corinthians 1:6.

> Every lesson you shall utter,
>   If the charge indeed be yours,
> First is gained by earnest learning,
> Carved in letters deep and burning,
>   On a heart that long endures.

— *February 9.* —

WHO shall be able to teach others also. Thou therefore endure hardness, as a good soldier of Jesus Christ.—2 Timothy 2:2, 3.

> He traineth thus
> That we may teach the lessons we are taught;
> That younger learners may be further brought,
>   Led on by us.
> Well may we wait, or toil, or suffer long,
> For His dear service so to be made fit and strong.

— *February 10.* —

UNTO you it is given in the behalf of Christ, not only to believe on Him, but also to suffer for His sake.—Philippians 1:29.

> O words of golden music,
>   Unknown to harps on high,
> Which find a tuneful anthem
>   Where we have found a sigh,
> And peal their holy praises
>   Just where ours faint and die.

— *February 11.* —

WHAT I do thou knowest not now; but thou shalt know hereafter.
—John 13:7.

Not yet thou knowest what I do,
O feeble child of earth,
Whose life is but to angel view
The morning of thy birth!
The smallest leaf, the simplest flower,
The wild bee's honey-cell,
Have lessons of My love and power
Too hard for thee to spell.

February 12.

No man can find out the work that God maketh from the beginning to the end.—Ecclesiastes 3:11.

That great scheme
Of which we, straining, catch a glimpse or gleam
In light or shadow;—scheme embracing all,
Star-system cycles, and the sparrow's fall;
Scheme all-combining, wisest, grandest, best.

February 13.

Thy thoughts which are to us-ward.—Psalm 40:5.

Each may deem
Himself a tiny centre of that thought;
For how mysteriously enwrought
Are all our moments in its folds of might,
Our own horizon ever bounding
And yet not limiting, but still surrounding
Our lives, while reaching far beyond our
quickest sight.

February 14.

Lo, these are parts of His ways: but how little a portion is heard of Him!—Job 26:14.

Then onward and yet onward, for the dim revealings show
That systems unto systems in grand succession grow;
That what we deemed a volume but one golden verse may be,
One rhythmic cadence in the flow of God's great poetry.

February 15.

IT is as high as heaven; what canst thou do? deeper than hell; what canst thou know?—Job 11:8.

Too wonderful for me.—Job 42:3.

> For thus our thoughts rebound
> From the Invisible-Infinite; on every side
> Hemmed ever round
> By the Impassable, that never mortal pinion
> Hath over-soared, that mocks at human pride,
> Imprisoned in its own supposed dominion.

February 16.

THOU art near, O Lord.—Psalm 119:151.

> I could not do without Thee,
> O Jesus, Saviour dear!
> E'en when mine eyes are holden,
> I know that Thou art near.
> How dreary and how lonely
> This changeful life would be
> Without the sweet communion,
> The secret rest with Thee!

February 17.

WE which have believed do enter into rest.—Hebrews 4:3.

> Resting 'neath His guiding Hand for untracked days,
> Resting 'neath His shadow, from the noontide rays,
> Resting at the eventide beneath His wing,
> In the fair pavilion of our Saviour-King.

February 18.

REST (*margin,* be silent) in the Lord, and wait patiently for Him.
—Psalm 37:7.

Rest and be silent! For, faithfully listening,
   Patiently waiting, thine eyes shall behold
Pearls in the waters of quietness glistening,
   Treasures of promise that He shall unfold.
Rest and be silent! for Jesus is here,
Calming and stilling each ripple of fear.

February 19.

THOU art the glory of their strength.—Psalm 89:17.
   With gladness and rejoicing shall they be brought.—Psalm 45:15.

In the Lord Jehovah trusting, everlasting strength have we;
He Himself, our Sun, our Glory. Everlasting Light shall be;
Everlasting life is ours, purchased by The Life laid down;
And our heads, oft bowed and weary, everlasting joy shall crown.

February 20.

BY grace are ye saved through faith; and that not of yourselves: it is
   the gift of God.—Ephesians 2:8.
Increase our faith.—Luke 17:5.

Increase our faith, belovèd Lord!
   For Thou alone canst give
The faith that takes Thee at Thy word,
   The faith by which we live.
Increase our faith! So weak are we,
   That we both may and must
Commit our very faith to Thee,
   Entrust to Thee our trust.

February 21.

SANCTIFIED by faith that is in me.—Acts 26:18.

Holiness by faith in Jesus, not by effort of thine own,—
Sin's dominion crushed and broken by the power of grace alone,—
God's own holiness within thee, His own beauty on thy brow,—
This shall be thy pilgrim brightness, this thy blessèd portion now.

February 22.

THAT we . . . may grow up into Him in all things.—Ephesians 4:14, 15.

> Let me, then, be always growing,
> Never, never standing still,
> Listening; learning, better knowing
> Thee and Thy most blessèd will.
> Till I reach Thy holy place,
> Daily let me grow in grace.

February 23.

I WILL betroth thee unto Me in righteousness, and in judgment, and in loving kindness, and in mercies. I will even betroth thee unto Me in faithfulness.—Hosea 2:19, 20.

> Therefore, justified for ever by the faith which He hath given,
> Peace, and joy, and hope abounding, smooth thy trial path to heaven:
> Unto Him betrothed for ever, who thy life shall crown and bless,
> By His name thou shalt be called, Christ, "The Lord our Righteousness!"

February 24.

St. Matthias.

I WOULD have you without carefulness.—1 Corinthians 7:32.
Casting all your care upon Him; for He careth for you.
—1 Peter 5:7.

> Without a shade of care,
> Because the Lord who loves us will every burden bear;
> Because we trust Him fully, and know that He will guide,
> And know that He will keep us at His belovèd side.

February 25.

THOU wilt keep him in perfect peace, whose mind is stayed on Thee: because he trusteth in Thee.—Isaiah 26:3.
Acquaint now thyself with Him, and be at peace.—Job 22:21.

> Stayed upon Jehovah,
> Hearts are fully blest,

Finding, *as He promised,*
Perfect peace and rest.

February 26.

Redemption through His blood.—Ephesians 1:7.

One thought, His thought of thoughts, awakes our song
Of endless thanks and marvelling adoration
More than aught else. For Providence, Creation,
All He hath made and all He doth prepare,
    Thoughts grand, and wise, and strong,
    Thoughts tender and most fair,
Are pale beside the glory of salvation,
Redemption's gracious plan and glorious revelation.

February 27.

The blood of Jesus Christ His Son cleanseth us from all sin.—1 John 1:7.
That He might sanctify the people with His own blood.
—Hebrews 13:12.

Precious, precious blood of Jesus,
    Let it make thee whole;
Let it flow in mighty cleansing o'er thy soul.
Though thy sins are red like crimson,
    Deep in scarlet glow,
Jesu's precious blood can make them white as snow.

February 28.

Only believe.—Mark 5:36.

While Reason, like a Levite, waits
    Where priest and people meet,
Faith, by "a new and living way,"
    Hath gained the mercy-seat.
While Reason but returns to tell
    That this is not our rest,
Faith, like a weary dove, hath sought
    A gracious Saviour's breast.

February 29.

WORKING in you that which is well-pleasing in His sight.
—Hebrews 13:21.

> Not yet thou knowest what I do
> Within thine own weak breast,
> To mould thee to My Image true,
> And fit thee for My rest.
> But yield thee to my loving skill;
> The veilèd work of grace,
> From day to day progressing still,
> It is not thine to trace.

MARCH.

———

HOSANNA! raise the pealing hymn
　　To David's Son and Lord;
With cherubim and seraphim
　　Exalt the Incarnate Word.

Hosanna! Lord, our feeble tongue
　　No lofty strains can raise:
But Thou wilt not despise the young,
　　Who meekly chant Thy praise.

Hosanna! Sovereign, Prophet, Priest;
　　How vast Thy gifts, how free!
Thy blood, our life; Thy word, our feast;
　　Thy name, our only plea.

Hosanna! Master, lo, we bring
　　Our offerings to Thy throne;
Nor gold, nor myrrh, nor mortal thing,
　　But hearts to be Thine own.

Hosanna! once Thy gracious ear
　　Approved a lisping throng:
Be gracious still, and deign to hear
　　Our poor but grateful song.

O Saviour, if redeemed by Thee,
　　Thy temple we behold,
Hosannas through eternity
　　We'll sing to harps of gold.

W. H. H.

March 1.

IN the morning sow thy seed, and in the evening withhold not thine hand: for thou knowest not whether shall prosper, either this or that, or whether they both shall be alike good.—Ecclesiastes 11:6.

In the morning sow thy seed, nor stay thy hand at evening hour,
Never asking which shall prosper—*both* may yield thee fruit and flower:
Thou shalt reap of that thou sowest, though thy grain be small and bare,
God shall clothe it as He pleases, for the harvest full and fair.

March 2.

IN whom we have redemption through His blood.—Ephesians 1:7.

Precious, precious blood of Jesus,
Shed on Calvary,
Shed for rebels, shed for sinners,
Shed for me!

Precious blood that hath redeemed us,
All the price is paid!
Perfect pardon now is offered,
Peace is made.

March 3.

I HAVE loved you, saith the Lord.—Malachi 1:2.

He hath loved thee, and He knows
All thy fears and all thy foes;
Victor thou shalt surely be
Ever through His love to thee.
Rest in quiet joy on this,—
Greater love hath none than His:
And may this thy life-song be,
Love to Him who loveth thee.

March 4.

BELIEVE on the Lord Jesus Christ, and thou shalt be saved.—Acts 16:31.

Fear not to trust His simple word,
So sweet, so tried, so true,
And you are safe for evermore,
Yes,—even you!

March 5.

H E is faithful and just to forgive us our sins, and to cleanse us.
—1 John 1:9.

That He might sanctify the people with His own blood.
—Hebrews 13:12.

I am trusting Thee for pardon, at Thy feet I bow;
For Thy grace and tender mercy, trusting now.
I am trusting Thee for cleansing, in the crimson flood;
Trusting Thee to make me holy, by Thy blood.

March 6.

I F we walk in the light, as He is in the light, we have fellowship one
with another, and the blood of Jesus Christ His Son cleanseth us from
all sin.—1 John 1:7.

Abiding in His presence, and walking in the light,
And seeking to " do always what is pleasing in His sight;"
We look to Him to keep us " all glorious within,"
Because " the blood of Jesus Christ *is cleansing* from all sin."

March 7.

B RINGING into captivity every thought to the obedience of Christ.
—2 Corinthians 10:5.

Let every thought
Be captive brought,
Lord Jesus Christ, to Thine own sweet obedience!
That I may know,
In ebbless flow,
The perfect peace of full and pure allegiance.

March 8.

WE love Him, because He first loved us.—1 John 4:19.

'Tis but a feeble echo of His great love to you,
Yet in His ear each note is clear, the harmony is true.
It is an uncut jewel, all earth-encrusted now,
But He will make it glorious, and set it on His brow.
'Tis but a tiny glimmer, lit from the Light above,
But it shall blaze through endless days, a star of perfect love.

March 9.

THE excellency of the knowledge of Christ Jesus my Lord.
—Philippians 3:8.

How real Thy mercy and Thy might!
How real Thy love, how real Thy light!
How real Thy truth and faithfulness!
How real Thy blessing when Thou dost bless!
How real Thy coming to dwell within!
How real the triumphs Thou dost win!
Does not the loving and glowing heart
Leap up to own how real Thou art!

March 10.

IN Thee do I put my trust. Blessed are all they that put their trust in Him.
—Psalm 7:1 ; 2:12.

I am trusting Thee, Lord Jesus,
Trusting only Thee!
Trusting Thee for full salvation,
Great and free.
I am trusting Thee, Lord Jesus,
Never let me fall!
I am trusting Thee for ever,
And for all.

March 11.

I HAVE many things to say unto you.—John 16:12.
Master, say on.—Luke 7:40.

Our own belovèd Master "hath many things to say,"
Look forward to His teaching, unfolding day by day;
To whispers of His Spirit, while resting at His feet,
To glowing revelation, to insight clear and sweet.

March 12.

THESE things I have spoken unto you, that in Me ye might have
peace. In the world ye shall have tribulation: but be of good cheer;
I have overcome the world.—John 16:33.

On the surface, foam and roar, restless heave and passionate dash,
Shingle rattle along the shore, gathering boom and thundering crash.
Under the surface, soft green light, a hush of peace and an endless calm,
Winds and waves from a choral height, falling sweet as a far-off psalm.

March 13.

THE Lord shall increase you more and more.—Psalm 115:14.
They shall increase as they have increased.—Zechariah 10:8.

Ever more and more bestowing,
Love and joy in riper glowing,
Faith increasing, graces growing,—
Such His promises to you!
He is faithful, He is true!

March 14.

I THE Lord do keep it; I will water it every moment: lest any hurt it, I
will keep it night and day.—Isaiah 27:3.

He will take care of you! yes, to the end!
He will not leave you one moment alone.
Oh, then, rejoice that you have such a Friend,
Nothing can alter His love to His own.

March 15.

THE Lord shall open unto thee His good treasure.—Deuteronomy 28:12.

> His love is the key, and His glory the measure
>   Of grace all-abounding and knowledge unpriced;
> To thee shall be opened this infinite treasure,
>   To thee the unsearchable riches of Christ!

March 16.

LOOK Thou upon me, and be merciful unto me, as Thou usest to do unto those that love Thy name.—Psalm 119:132.

And the Lord looked upon him, and said, Go in this thy might.—Judges 6:14.

> I should not love Thee now wert Thou not near,
> Looking on me in love. Look on me still,
> Lord Jesus Christ, and let Thy look give strength
> To work for Thee with single heart and eye.

March 17.

THE desire of our soul is to Thy name.—Isaiah 26:8.
Let them also that love Thy name be joyful in Thee.—Psalm 5:11.

> Now I know Thy Name,
> Its mighty music is the only key
> To which my soul vibrates in full accord;
> Blending with other notes but as they blend
> With this.

March 18.

O THE depth of the riches both of the wisdom and knowledge of God! how unsearchable are His judgments, and His ways past finding out!—Romans 11:33.

> The very faith that brings us near
> Reveals new distances, new depths of light

Unfathomed,—seas of suns that never eye
Created hath beheld or can behold.

March 19.

THOU hast put gladness in my heart. The secret of the Lord is with them that fear Him.—Psalm 4:7 ; Psalm 25:14.

> Thou hast put gladness in my heart,
>   Then well may I be glad!
> Without the secret of Thy love,
>   I could not but be sad.
> O Master, gracious Master,
>   What will Thy presence be,
> If such a thrill of joy can crown
>   One upward look to Thee!

March 20.

WHERE I am, there shall also my servant be.—John 12:26.

> Our fairest dream can never
>   Outshine that holy light,
> Our noblest thought can never soar
>   Beyond that Word of might.
> Our whole anticipation,
>   Our Master's best reward,
> Our crown of bliss, is summed in this—
>   "For ever with the Lord!"

March 21.

I WILL declare Thy name unto my brethren, in the midst of the church will I sing praise unto Thee.—Hebrews 2:12.

> With perfect praise,
> With interchange of rapturous revelation
> From Christ Himself, the burning adoration
>   Yet higher to raise,
> For ever and for ever so to bring
> More glory and still more, to Him, our gracious King!

— *March 22.* —

THE cup which My Father hath given Me, shall I not drink it?
—John 18:11.
My cup runneth over.—Psalm 23:5.

> He drank the cup of sorrows,
> But mine runs o'er
> With faithfulness and mercy,
> And love's sweet store.

— *March 23.* —

BUT He was wounded for our transgressions, He was bruised for our
iniquities: the chastisement of our peace was upon Him; and with
His stripes we are healed.—Isaiah 53:5.

> Thine was the chastisement, with no release,
>   That mine might be the peace;
> The bruising and the cruel stripes were Thine,
>   That healing might be mine;
> Thine was the sentence and the condemnation,
> Mine the acquittal, and the full salvation.

— *March 24.* —

THE eternal purpose which He purposed in Christ Jesus our Lord.
—Ephesians 3:11.

> O thought of consummated melody
> And perfect rhythm! though its mighty beat
> Transcend angelic faculty, and though its mighty bars
> May be the fall of worlds, the birth of stars,
> Its measure—all eternity—one echo, calm and sweet,
> Our clue to this great music of God's plan,
>   Sounds on in ever-varying repeat—
> Glory to God on high, peace and goodwill to man.

— *March 25.* —

Annunciation of the Virgin Mary.

WHO was delivered for our offences, and was raised again for our
justification. Therefore being justified by faith, we have peace
with God through our Lord Jesus Christ.—Romans 4:25; 5:1.

By the grace of God the Father, thou art freely justified,
Through the great redemption purchased by the blood of Him who died;
By His life, for thee fulfilling God's command exceeding broad,
By His glorious resurrection, seal and signet of thy God.

March 26.

IF our transgressions and our sins be upon us, and we pine away in them, how should we then live?—Ezekiel 33:10.
The Lord hath laid on Him the iniquity of us all.—Isaiah 53:6.

On Thee, the Lord
My mighty sins hath laid;
And against Thee Jehovah's sword
Flashed forth its fiery blade.
The stroke of justice fell on Thee,
That it might never fall on me.

March 27.

SAVED in the Lord with an everlasting salvation.—Isaiah 45:17.

With salvation everlasting He shall save us, He shall bless
With the largess of Messiah, everlasting righteousness;
Ours the everlasting mercy all His wondrous dealings prove;
Ours His everlasting kindness, fruit of everlasting love.

March 28.

THAT I may know Him, and the power of His resurrection.
—Philippians 3:10.

Oh, let me know
The power of Thy resurrection!
Oh, let me show
Thy risen life in clear reflection!
Oh, let me soar
Where Thou, my Saviour Christ, art gone before!
In mind and heart,
Let me dwell always, only where Thou art.

March 29.

Unto every one that hath shall be given, and he shall have abundance.—Matthew 25:29.

Unto him that hath, Thou givest
Ever more abundantly;
Lord, I live because Thou livest,
Therefore give more life to me,
Therefore speed me in the race,
Therefore let me grow in grace.

March 30.

Thine age shall be clearer than the noonday,—Job 11:17.

Fear not the westering shadows,
O children of the Day!
For brighter still, and brighter
Shall be your homeward way.
Resplendent as the morning,
With fuller glow and power,
And clearer than the noonday
Shall be your sunset hour.

March 31.

That the life also of Jesus might be made manifest in our mortal flesh.
—2 Corinthians 4:11.

Thy life in me be shown!
Lord, I would henceforth seek
To think and speak
Thy thoughts, Thy words alone,
No more my own.

APRIL.

_____

ALL hail, Thou Resurrection!
  All hail, Thou Life and Light!
All hail, Thou Self-Perfection,
  Sole source of grace and might!
Thy Church, O Christ, now greets Thee,
  Uprising from the grave,
And every eye that meets Thee
  Beholds Thee strong to save.

All hail, belovèd Jesus!
  For Thou indeed art He
Whose death from sin now frees us,
  Whose life brings liberty.
Hence let our faith embrace Thee
  With warmest hand and eye,
And then delight to trace Thee
  Ascending up on high.

O Saviour, come in glory
  To raise Thy holy dead,
And end redemption's story,
  With crowns upon Thy head.
Then robed in white before Thee,
  Without one stain or tear,
Shall all Thy saints adore Thee,
  'Midst wonder, love and fear.

_W. H. H._

April 1.

THIS is a faithful saying, and worthy of all acceptation, that Christ Jesus came into the world to save sinners.—1 Timothy 1:15.

He came to bring the weary ones
True peace and perfect rest;
To take away the guilt and sin
Which darkened and distressed;
That great and small might hear His call,
And all be saved and blessed.

April 2.

I HELD Him, and would not let Him go.—Song of Solomon 3:4.
Fear not: for I have redeemed thee.—Isaiah 43:1.

I could not do without Thee,
O Saviour of the lost!
Whose precious blood redeemed me
At such tremendous cost.
Thy righteousness, Thy pardon,
Thy precious blood, must be
My only hope and comfort,
My glory and my plea.

April 3.

WHO His own self bare our sins in His own body on the tree, that we, being dead to sins, should live unto righteousness: by whose stripes ye were healed.—1 Peter 2:24.

Wounded for my transgression, stricken sore,
That I might "sin no more;"
Weak, that I might be always strong in Thee,
Bound, that I might be free;
Acquaint with grief, that I might only know
Fulness of joy in everlasting flow.

April 4.

HIS great love wherewith He loved us.—Ephesians 2:4.

O love surpassing thought,
So bright, so grand, so clear, so true, so glorious;
Love infinite, love tender, love unsought,
Love changeless, love rejoicing, love victorious:
And this great love for us, in boundless store:
God's everlasting love! What would we more!

April 5.

I AM come that they might have life, and that they might have it more abundantly.—John 10:10.

The blest reality
Of resurrection-power,
Thy Church's dower,
Life more abundantly,
Lord, give to me.

April 6.

WE shall be like Him; for we shall see Him as He is.—1 John 3:2.

What a change has passed upon them!
Made like Him, the Perfect One,—
Made like Him, whose Joy they enter,
Him, the only Crown and Centre
Of the endless bliss begun.

April 7.

CHRIST hath redeemed us from the curse of the law, being made a curse for us.—Galatians 3:13.

What hast Thou done for me, O mighty Friend,
Who lovest to the end?
Reveal Thyself, that I may now behold
Thy love unknown, untold,
Bearing the curse, and made a curse for me,
That blessed and made a blessing I might be.

April 8.

I FOUND Him whom my soul loveth.—Song of Solomon 3:4.

> Through the dim storm a white peace-bearing Dove
>   Gleams, and the mist rolls back, the shadows flee,
> The night is past. A clear, calm sky above,
>   Firm rock beneath; a royal-scrollèd tree,
> And One, thorn-diademed, the King of Love,
>   The Son of God who gave Himself for me.

April 9.

I F we have been planted together in the likeness of His death, we shall be also in the likeness of His resurrection.—Romans 6:5.

> In the likeness of His death
>   We were planted;
> Therefore, by His Spirit's breath,
>   Resurrection-life is granted;—
> Resurrection-beauty glowing,
> Resurrection-power outflowing,
> Resurrection-gladness cheering,
> Resurrection-glory nearing.

April 10.

U NTO Him that loved us, and washed us from our sins in His own blood, and hath made us kings and priests unto God and His Father; to Him be glory and dominion for ever and ever.—Revelation 1:5, 6.

> Glory be to Him who loved us,
>   And redeemed us unto God!
> New and living revelation
> Of the marvels of salvation,
> Wakes new depths of adoration,
>   New and burning laud.

April 11.

CHRIST also hath once suffered for sins, the just for the unjust.
—1 Peter 3:18.

> For Thee, revilings and the mocking throng,
>   For me, the angels' song;
> For Thee, the frown, the hiding of God's face,
>   For me, His smile of grace;
> Sorrows of hell and bitterest death for Thee,
> And heaven and everlasting life for me.

April 12.

YOUR life is hid with Christ in God.—Colossians 3:3.

> Jesus, my life is Thine,
> And evermore shall be
> Hidden in Thee,
> For nothing can untwine
> Thy life from mine.

April 13.

O DEATH, where is thy sting? O grave, where is thy victory?
—1 Corinthians 15:55.

> Rest, by His sorrow! Bruisèd for our sin,
>   Behold the Lamb of God! His death, our life.
> Now lift your heads, ye gates! He entereth in,
>   Christ risen indeed, and Conqueror in the strife.
> Thanks, thanks to Him who won, and Him who gave
> Such victory of love, such triumph o'er the grave.

April 14.

WE will remember Thy love.—Song of Solomon 1:4.
Thou meetest . . . those that remember Thee.—Isaiah 64:5.

> Our Master's love remember,
>   Exceeding great and free;
> Lift up thy heart in gladness,
>   For He remembers thee.

April 15.

THOU wast slain, and hast redeemed us to God by Thy blood.
—Revelation 5:9.

> "Not your own!" but His ye are,
>   Who hath paid a price untold
> For your life, exceeding far
>   All earth's store of gems and gold.
> With the precious blood of Christ,
> Ransom treasure all unpriced,
> Full redemption is procured,
> Free salvation is assured.

April 16.

THEY overcame him by the blood of the Lamb.—Revelation 12:11.

> Precious blood! by this we conquer
>   In the fiercest fight;
> Sin and Satan overcoming
>   By its might.

April 17.

THIS is the day which the Lord hath made, we will rejoice and be glad
in it.—Psalm 118:24.

> Rejoice and be glad as ye sing,
>   For the Day of our Saviour and King,
> The Life that is risen, the Truth and the Way!
>   Salvation He brought us,
>   When wandering he sought us,
>   With blood He hath bought us,
>   O, praise Him to-day!

April 18.

YE call Me Master and Lord: and ye say well; for so I am.
—John 13:13.

O Master, at Thy feet
I bow in rapture sweet;
Before me as in darkling glass,
Some glorious outlines pass
Of love, and truth, and holiness, and power;
I own them Thine, O Christ, and bless Thee for this hour.

April 19.

THEY shall sorrow a little for the burden of the King of princes.
—Hosea 8:10.

O Thou wast crowned with thorns, that I might wear
A crown of glory fair,
Exceeding sorrowful, that I might be
Exceeding glad in Thee;
Rejected and despised, that I might stand
Accepted and complete at Thy right hand.

April 20.

THOU shalt abide for Me many days; . . . so will I also be for thee.
—Hosea 3:3.

My life I bring to Thee,
I would not be my own;
O Saviour, let me be
Thine ever, Thine alone.
My heart, my life, my all I bring
To Thee, my Saviour and my King.

April 21.

HE is risen, as He said.—Matthew 28:6.
Arise, shine; for thy light is come, and the glory of the Lord is
risen upon thee.—Isaiah 60:1.

Arise! for He is risen to-day;
And shine, for He is glorified!
Put on thy beautiful array,
And keep perpetual Eastertide.

April 22.

AWAKE and sing, ye that dwell in dust. Shake thyself from the dust; arise!—Isaiah 26:19; 52:2.

> Awake, awake!
> For life is sweet;
> Awake, awake!
> New hopes to greet.
> The shadows are fleeting,
> The substance is sure;
> The joys thou art meeting
> Shall ever endure.

April 23.

THE love of Christ constraineth us.—2 Corinthians 5:14.

> Thy Cross and Passion and Thy precious death,
> While I have mortal breath,
> Shall be my spring of love and work and praise,
> The life of all my days;
> Till all this mystery of Love supreme
> Be solved in glory, glory's endless theme.

April 24.

THESE things have I spoken unto you, that My joy might remain in you.—John 15:11.

> O joy abiding and divine!
> Not mine at all, but Thine,
> Or else not any joy to me!
> For a joy that flowed not from Thine own
> Since Thou hast reigned alone,
> Were vacancy or misery.

April 25.

St. Mark.

SHEW Thy marvellous lovingkindness. Shine forth.—Psalm 17:7; 80:1.

O Saviour, precious Saviour, come in all Thy power and grace,
And take away the veil that hides the brightness of Thy face!
Oh, manifest the marvels of Thy tenderness and love,
And let Thy Name be blessed and praised all other names above.

April 26.

A TRIED Stone.—Isaiah 28:16.

Through the yesterday of ages,
    Jesus! Thou hast been the same!
Through our own life's chequered pages,
    Still the one, dear, changeless Name.
Well may we in Thee confide,
Faithful Saviour, proved and tried.

April 27.

A PRECIOUS Corner Stone.—Isaiah 28:16.
He is precious.—1 Peter 2:7.

Joyfully we stand and witness,
    Thou art still to-day the same,
In Thy perfect, glorious fitness
    Meeting every need and claim.
Chiefest of ten thousand Thou!
Saviour, O most precious now!

April 28.

A SURE Foundation.—Isaiah 28:16.
Jesus Christ, the same yesterday, and to-day, and for ever.
—Hebrews 13:8.

Gazing down the far For Ever,
    Brighter glows the one sweet Name;
Stedfast radiance, paling never,
    Jesus, Jesus! still the same.
Evermore Thou shalt endure,
Our own Saviour, strong and sure.

—————————— *April 29.* ——————————

THEY go from strength to strength.—Psalm 84:7.

Though we know there may be tempests, and we know there will be showers,
Yet we know they only hasten summer's richer crown of flowers.
Blossom leads to golden fruitage, bursting bud to foliage soon,
April's pleasant gleam shall strengthen to the glorious glow of June.

—————————— *April 30.* ——————————

THE Lord shall increase you more and more.—Psalm 115:14.
They shall increase as they have increased.—Zechariah 10:8.

So we look in faith and gladness for the summer days in store,
For the treasures and the glories that shall open more and more;
So the silver carol rises, for the winter time in past!
When the summertide is coming, need we ask if spring shall last?

MAY.

———

REMEMBER, Lord, Thy word of old,
 The promised flood of grace;
When earth Thy blessing shall behold,
 As streams in every place.

The barren wild and thirsty soil,
 Thy Spirit, Lord, await;
O pour it forth, and crown our toil
 In every heathen gate!

Where thorns and briars choke the ground,
 And withering idols reign,
There let Thy Spirit's dew abound,
 And Eden bloom again.

O Holy Ghost, on every heart,
 In every land descend!
Thy fertilising gifts impart,
 And bring a glorious end.

Thee, with the Father and the Son,
 Thy sainted hosts shall praise,
Those hosts by Thee in Christ made one,
 For everlasting days.

W. H. H.

May 1.

St. Philip and St. James.

No man can come to Me, except the Father which hath sent Me draw him.—John 6:44.

With lovingkindness have I drawn thee.—Jeremiah 31:3.

> From no less fountain such a stream could flow,
> No other root could yield so fair a flower;
> Had He not loved, He had not drawn us so;
> Had He not drawn, we had nor will nor power
> To rise, to come;—the Saviour had passed by,
> Where we in blindness sat without one care or cry.

May 2.

Thou shalt be called, Sought out.—Isaiah 62:12.

Now in Christ Jesus ye who sometimes were far off are made nigh by the blood of Christ.—Ephesians 2:13.

> Father, we bless Thee with heart and voice
> For the wondrous grace of Thy sovereign choice,
> That patiently, gently, sought us out
> In the far-off land of death and doubt,
> That drew us to Christ by the Spirit's might,
> That opened our eyes to see the light
> > That arose in strange reality
> From the darkness that fell on Calvary.

May 3.

Whosoever drinketh of this water shall thirst again: but whosoever drinketh of the water that I shall give him shall never thirst. Sir, give me this water.—John 4:13–15.

> A heart where emptiness seemed emptier made
> > By colourless remains of tasteless pleasure;
> ONE came, and, pitying the hollow shade,
> > Poured in His own strong love in fullest measure;
> Illumined it with His own radiant light,
> > And stilled it with the Presence of His might.

May 4.

O taste and see that the Lord is good: blessed is the man that trusteth in him.—Psalm 34:8.

Come and see!—John 1:46.

I could not do without Him!
  Jesus is more to me
Than all the richest, fairest gifts
  Of earth could ever be.
But the more I find Him precious,
  And the more I find Him true,
The more I long for you to find
  What He can be to you.

May 5.

WITH Me where I am.—John 17:24.

But with Him—oh! *with Jesus!*
  Are any words so blest?
With Jesus, everlasting joy
  And everlasting rest!
With Jesus—all the empty heart
  Filled with His perfect love;
With Jesus—perfect peace below,
  And perfect bliss above.

May 6.

HIM hath God exalted with His right hand to be a Prince and a Saviour.—Acts 5:31.

He who came to save us
  He who bled and died,
Now is crowned with glory
  At His Father's side.
Never more to suffer,
  Never more to die,
Jesus, King of glory,
  Is gone up on high.

May 7.

I GO to prepare a place for you.—John 14:2.

Praying for His children
  In that blessèd place,
Calling them to glory,
  Sending them His grace;
His bright home preparing,
  Faithful ones for you;
Jesus ever liveth,
  Ever loveth too.

May 8.

Seeing He ever liveth to make intercession for them.—Hebrews 7:25.

For while one weary child of His yet wanders here below,
And while one thirsting heart desires His peace and love to know,
And while one fainting spirit seeks His holiness to share,
The Saviour's mighty heart shall pour a tide of mighty prayer.

May 9.

Because I live, ye shall live also.—John 14:19.

I give unto them eternal life; and they shall never perish, neither shall any man pluck them out of My hand.—John 10:28.

Everlasting life Thou givest,
    Everlasting love to see;
They shall live because Thou livest,
    And their life is hid with Thee.
Safe Thy members shall be found,
When their glorious Head is crowned!

May 10.

Rejoice, inasmuch as ye are partakers of Christ's sufferings; that, when His glory shall be revealed, ye may be glad also with exceeding joy.—1 Peter 4:13.

O the rapture of that vision!
    (Every earthly passion o'er,)
Our Redeemer's coronation,
And the blissful exaltation
    Of the dear ones gone before.
        Grace that shone for Christ below,
        Changed to glory we shall know.

May 11.

What shall I render unto the Lord for all His benefits toward me?
—Psalm 116:12.

What hast thou that thou didst not receive?—1 Corinthians 4:7.

What shall I render to my glorious King?
  I have but that which I receive from Thee;
  And what I give Thou givest back to me.
Transmuted by Thy touch, each worthless thing
Changed to the preciousness of gem or gold,
And by Thy blessing multiplied a thousand-fold.

May 12.

H E is Lord of lords and King of kings; and they that are with Him are called, and chosen, and faithful.—Revelation 17:14.

True-hearted, whole-hearted! Faithful and loyal,
  King of our lives, by Thy grace we will be!
Under Thy standard, exalted and royal,
  Strong in Thy strength we will battle for Thee!

True-hearted, whole-hearted! Fullest allegiance
  Yielding henceforth to our glorious King!
Valiant endeavour and loving obedience
  Freely and joyously now would we bring.

May 13.

N O man can say that Jesus is the Lord, but by the Holy Ghost.
  —1 Corinthians 12:3.

My Lord! My heart hath said it joyfully!
Nay, could it be my own cold, treacherous heart?
'Tis comfort to remember that we have
Nor will nor power to think one holy thought,
And thereby estimate His power in us.

May 14.

B LESSING, and honour, and glory, and power be unto Him.
  —Revelation 5:13.

Hallelujahs full and swelling
  Rise around His throne of might.
All our highest laud excelling,
Holy and immortal, dwelling
  In the unapproachèd light,
He is worthy to receive
All that heaven and earth can give,
Blessing, honour, glory, might,
All are His by glorious right.

May 15.

OF the increase of His government and peace there shall be no end.
—Isaiah 9:7.

> Thy reign shall still increase.
> I claim Thy word!
> Let righteousness and peace
> And joy yet more and more abound
> In me, through Thee, O Christ my Lord.
> Take unto Thee Thy power, who art
> My Sovereign, Many-Crowned!
> 'Stablish Thy Kingdom in my heart.

May 16.

SO the Lord shall make bright clouds, and give them showers of rain.
—Zechariah 10:1.

He shall come unto us as the rain.—Hosea 6:3.

> On every budding leaf and flower
> The sweet, soft rain of spring
> Comes down in a gentle, whispering shower,
> Like the passing of angel-wing.
> There is a rain for the waiting soul,
> A sweet and refreshing dew,
> A Spirit who makes the wounded whole,
> And the evil heart makes new.

May 17.

I WILL water it every moment.—Isaiah 27:3.

> Let me grow by sun and shower,
> Every moment water me;
> Make me really, hour by hour,
> More and more conformed to Thee,
> That Thy loving eye may trace
> Day by day my growth in grace.

May 18.

LET everything that hath breath praise the Lord. Hallelujah.
—Psalm 150:6.

> Hark! "Hallelujah!" O sublimest strain!
> Is it prophetic echo of the day

When He, our Saviour and our King, shall reign,
　And all the earth shall own His righteous sway?
Lift heart and voice, and swell the mighty chords,
While hallelujahs peal to Him, the Lord of lords.

May 19.

AND He shall reign for ever and ever.—Revelation 11:15.

　　O the joy to see Thee reigning,
　　　Thee, my own belovèd Lord!
　　Every tongue Thy name confessing,
　　Worship, honour, glory, blessing,
　　　Brought to Thee with glad accord!
　　Thee, my Master, and my Friend,
　　　Vindicated and enthroned!
　　Unto earth's remotest end
　　　Glorified, adored, and owned!

May 20.

DAILY shall He be praised.—Psalm 72:15.
I will yet praise Thee more and more.—Psalm 71:14

　　We need not wait for earthquake, storm, and fire,
　　　To lift our praises higher;
　　Nor wait for heaven-dawn ere we join the hymn
　　　Of throne-surrounding cherubim;
　　We know the still, small Voice, in many a word
　　Of guidance and command and promise heard,
　　And, knowing it, we bow before His feet,
　　With love and awe the seraph-strain repeat.

May 21.

UNTO Him that loved us . . . be glory and dominion for ever and ever.
Amen.—Revelation 1:5, 6.

　　　As the sound of many waters
　　　　Let the full Amen arise!
　　　HALLELUJAH! Ceasing never,
　　　Sounding through the great FOR EVER,
　　　　Linking all in harmonies;
　　　Through eternities of bliss,
　　　Lord, our rapture shall be this;
　　　And our endless life shall be
　　　One AMEN of praise to Thee.

———— *May 22.* ————

I HAVE glorified Thee on the earth: I have finished the work which Thou gavest me to do.—John 17:4.

> All His work is ended,
> Joyfully we sing!
> Jesus hath ascended,
> Glory to our King!

———— *May 23.* ————

How excellent is Thy name!—Psalm 8:1. How excellent is Thy lovingkindness!—Psalm 36:7.

> O Lord, our Lord! how excellent Thy Name
> Throughout this universal frame!
> Therefore Thy children rest
> Beneath the shadow of Thy wings,
> A shelter safe and blest,
> And tune their often tremulous strings,
> Thy love to praise, Thy glory to proclaim,
> The Merciful, the Gracious One, eternally the same.

———— *May 24.* ————

BECAUSE the Lord hath loved His people, He hath made Thee King over them.—2 Chronicles 2:11.

> O, blessed be the Lord thy God, who set
> Our King upon His throne; Divine delight
> In the Belovèd, crowning Thee with might,
> Honour, and majesty supreme; and yet
> The strange and godlike secret opening thus—
> The Kingship of His Christ ordained through love to us!

———— *May 25.* ————

WHEN the enemy shall come in like a flood, the Spirit of the Lord shall lift up a standard against him.—Isaiah 59:19.

Blessèd Spirit, lift Thy Standard,
   Pour Thy grace and shed Thy light!
Lift the veil and loose the fetter,
   Come with new and quickening might.
Make the desert places blossom,
   Shower Thy sevenfold gifts abroad,
Make Thy servants wise and stedfast,
   Valiant for the truth of God.

May 26.

WHOM have I in heaven but Thee? and there is none upon earth that I desire beside Thee.—Psalm 73:25.

"He is thy Lord!" Thyself, O Saviour dear,
And not another. Whom have I but Thee
In heaven or earth? and whom should I desire?
For Thou hast said, "So shall the King desire thee!"
And well may I respond in wondering love,
"Thou art my Lord, and I will worship Thee."

May 27.

MINE, . . . in that day when I make up My jewels.—Malachi 3:17.

"Not your own!" but His by right,
   His peculiar treasure now,
Fair and precious in His sight,
   Purchased jewels for His brow.
He will keep what thus He sought,
Safely guard the dearly bought,
Cherish that which He did choose,
Always love and never lose.

May 28.

I WILL pour water upon him that is thirsty, and floods upon the dry ground: I will pour My spirit upon thy seed, and My blessing upon thine offspring.—Isaiah 44:3.

Thine, O Christian, is this treasure, to thy risen Head assured!
Thine in full and gracious measure, thine by covenant secured!
Now arise! His word possessing, claim the promise of the Lord;
Plead through Christ for showers of blessing, till the Spirit be outpoured!

May 29.

THE earnest of the Spirit in our hearts.—2 Corinthians 1:22.

Oh, this is more than poem,
And more than highest song,
A witness with our spirit,
Though hidden, full and strong.
'Tis no new revelation
Vouchsafed to saint or sage,
But light from God cast bright and broad
Upon the sacred page.

May 30.

HIS glory is great in Thy salvation: honour and majesty hast Thou laid upon Him.—Psalm 21:5.

Golden harps are sounding,
Angel voices ring,
Pearly gates are opened,
Opened for the King.
Christ, the King of Glory,
Jesus, King of Love,
Is gone up in triumph
To His throne above.

May 31.

ELECT according to the foreknowledge of God the Father, through sanctification of the Spirit, unto obedience and sprinkling of the blood of Jesus Christ.—1 Peter 1:2.

To Him be glory and dominion for ever and ever. Amen.
—1 Peter 5:11.

O Love that chose, O Love that died,
O Love that sealed and sanctified,
All glory, glory, glory be,
O Covenant, Triune God, to Thee.

JUNE.

———

SUMMER-TIDE is coming,
    With all its pleasant things;
Every bee is humming,
    And every songster sings.
Mornings now are brightsome,
    Inviting student thought;
Evenings, too, are lightsome,
    With balmy quiet fraught.
Hearths no longer lure us,
    The fields instead we roam;
Hearts albeit insure us
    A happy, happy home.

Summer-tide, I hail thee,
    The empress of the year!
But thou soon wouldst fail me,
    Were not thy Maker near.
He thy course disposes,
    Thy light, thy scent, thy glow;
He tints all thy roses,
    And paints thy brilliant bow.
Laud Him, all creation,
    The sinner's mighty Friend;
Near Him be our station,
    Where summer ne'er shall end.

W. H. H.

June 1.

Eye hath not seen, nor ear heard, neither have entered into the heart of man, the things which God hath prepared for them that love Him. But God hath revealed them unto us by His Spirit.—1 Corinthians 2:9, 10.

> For angel-echoes reach us, borne on from star to star,
> And glimpses of our purchased home not always faint and far.
> No harp seraphic brings them, no poet's glowing word,
> By One alone revealed and known—the Spirit of the Lord.

June 2.

I shall be satisfied, when I awake, with Thy likeness.—Psalm 17:15.

> For infinite outpourings of Jehovah's love and grace,
> And infinite unveilings of the brightness of His face.
> And infinite unfoldings of the splendour of His will,
> Meet the mightiest expansions of the finite spirit still.

June 3.

My peace I give unto you.—John 14:27.

> Thy Reign is perfect Peace,
> Not mine, but Thine!
> A stream that shall not cease,
> For its fountain is Thy heart! O depth unknown!
> Thou givest of Thine own,
> Pouring from Thine and filling mine.

June 4.

His Name shall endure for ever. Blessed be His glorious Name. —Psalm 72:17, 19.

> All Thy glories are eternal,
> None shall ever pass away;
> Truth and mercy all-victorious,
> Righteousness and love all-glorious,
> Shine with everlasting ray:

All-resplendent, ere the light
Bade primeval darkness flee;
All-transcendent, through the flight
Of eternities to be.

June 5.

Having received of the Father the promise of the Holy Ghost, He hath shed forth this.—Acts 2:33.
And again they say, Alleluia.—Revelation 19:3.

To Thee, whose faithful love had place
In God's great covenant of grace;
To Thee, by Jesus Christ sent down,
Of all His gifts the sum and crown;
To Thee, who art with God the Son
And God the Father ever One, sing we Alleluia!

June 6.

In whom also after that ye believed, ye were sealed with that holy Spirit of promise, which is the earnest of our inheritance.—Ephesians 1:13, 14.

To Thee, whose faithful power doth heal,
Enlighten, sanctify, and seal—
To Thee whose Faithful truth is shown
By every promise made our own,
Sing we Alleluia.

June 7.

God was manifest in the flesh.—1 Timothy 3:16.
This God is our God for ever and ever.—Psalm 48:14.

King of Eternity! what revelation
Could the created and finite sustain,
But for Thy marvellous manifestation,
Godhead incarnate in weakness and pain!
Therefore archangels and angels adore Thee.
Cherubims wonder, and seraphs admire;
Therefore we praise Thee, rejoicing before Thee,
Joining in rapture the heavenly choir.

June 8.

THERE was a rainbow round about the throne, in sight like unto an emerald.—Revelation 4:3.

Oh, surround Thy throne of power with Thine emerald bow of peace;
Bid the wailing and the warring and the wild confusion cease.
Thou remainest King for ever, Thou shalt reign, and earth adore!
Thine the kingdom, Thine the power, Thine the glory evermore.

June 9.

THE Spirit itself beareth witness with our spirit, that we are the children of God.—Romans 8:16.

Like stars that tremble into light
Out of the purple dark, a low, sweet note
Just trembled out of silence, antidote
To any doubt; for never finger might
Produce that note, so different, so new:
Melodious pledge that all He promised should come true.

June 10.

THE Spirit also helpeth our infirmities.—Romans 8:26.

He will teach the trembling one to cling
To an arm of love and might;
And the earth-stained soul 'neath His holy wing
Shall be made all pure and white.
The anxious heart with its wild unrest
He can hush to a trustful calm;
To the spirit broken and depressed
He cometh with healing balm.

June 11.

St. Barnabas.

As one whom his mother comforteth, so will I comfort you; and ye shall be comforted.—Isaiah 66:13.

As gentlest touch will stay
The strong vibrations of a jarring chord,
So lay Thy hand upon his heart, and still
Each overstraining throb, each pulsing pain;
Then, in the stillness, breathe upon the strings,
And let Thy holy music overflow
With soothing power his listening, resting soul.

June 12.

COMFORT ye, comfort ye My people, saith your God.—Isaiah 40:1.

May He who taught the morning stars to sing,
Aye keep my chalice cool, and pure, and sweet;
And grant me so with loving hand to bring
Refreshment to His weary ones, to meet
Their thirst with water from God's music-spring;
And bearing thus, to pour it at His feet.

June 13.

THE comfort of the Holy Ghost.—Acts 9:31.
Thy Spirit is good; lead me.—Psalm 143:10.
Thou gavest also Thy good Spirit to instruct them.—Nehemiah 9:20.

To Thee, O Comforter Divine,
For all Thy grace and power benign,
To Thee, our Teacher and our Friend,
Our faithful Leader in the end,
Sing we Alleluia.

June 14.

THIS is the will of God, even your sanctification. —1 Thessalonians 4:3.

By His will He sanctifieth, by the Spirit's power within;
By the loving Hand that chasteneth fruits of righteousness to win;
By His truth and by His promise, by the Word, His gift unpriced,
By His own blood, and by union with the risen life of Christ.

--- *June 15.* ---

I KNOW the thoughts that I think toward you, saith the Lord, thoughts of peace, and not of evil.—Jeremiah 29:11.

As we lean upon His breast,
There, there we find a point of perfect rest
And glorious safety. There we see
His thoughts to usward, thoughts of peace,
That stoop in tenderest love; that still increase
With increase of our need; that never change,
That never fail, or falter, or forget.

--- *June 16.* ---

FROM everlasting to everlasting, Thou art God.—Psalm 90:2.

Thou art God from everlasting,
And to everlasting art;
Ere the dawn of shadowy ages,
Dimly guessed by angel-sages,
Ere the beat of seraph-heart;
Thou, Jehovah, art the same,
And Thy years shall have no end;
Changeless nature, changeless name,
Ever Father, God, and Friend.

--- *June 17.* ---

ALL Thy works shall praise Thee, O Lord; and Thy saints shall bless Thee.
—Psalm 145:10.

A praise that we are sharing
With every singing breeze,
With nightingales and linnets,
With waterfalls and trees;
With anthems of the flowers,
Too delicate and sweet
For all their fairy minstrelsy
Our mortal ears to greet.

--- *June 18.* ---

THE path of the just is as the shining light, that shineth more and more unto the perfect day.—Proverbs 4:18.

Each Amen becomes an anthem, for we know He will fulfil
All the purpose of His goodness, all the splendour of His will;
Only trust the living Saviour, only trust Him all the way,
And your springtide path shall brighten to the perfect summer day.

June 19.

THOU shalt guide me with Thy counsel, and afterward receive me to glory.—Psalm 73:24.

> Now, the long and toilsome duty
>   Stone by stone to carve and bring;
> Afterward, the perfect beauty
>   Of the palace of the King.
>
> Now, the tuning and the tension,
>   Wailing minors, discord strong;
> Afterward, the grand ascension
>   Of the Alleluia song.

June 20.

O LORD my God, Thou art very great.—Psalm 104:1.
Glorious in holiness, fearful in praises.—Exodus 15:11.

> Holy and Infinite! limitless, boundless,
>   All Thy perfections and powers and praise!
> Ocean of mystery! awful and soundless
>   All Thine unsearchable judgments and ways.
> Glorious in holiness, fearful in praises,
>   Who shall not fear Thee, and who shall not laud;
> Anthems of glory Thy universe raises,
>   Holy and Infinite! Father and God!

June 21.

MY thoughts are not your thoughts.—Isaiah 55:8.

> And now, search fearlessly
> The imperfections and obscurity,
>   The weakness and impurity
> Of all our thoughts. On each discovery
> Write "NOT as ours!" Then in every line
>   Behold God's glory shine
> In humbling, yet sweet contrast, as we view
> *His* thoughts, Eternal, Strong and Holy, Infinite and True.

--- *June 22.* ---

Blessed are all they that wait for Him.—Isaiah 30:18.

> When a sudden sorrow
>   Comes like cloud and night,
> Wait for God's to-morrow,
>   All will then be bright.
> Only wait and trust Him
>   Just a little while,
> After evening tear-drops
>   Shall come the morning smile.

--- *June 23.* ---

In His favour is life: weeping may endure for a night, but joy cometh in the morning.—Psalm 30:5.

> Sadly bend the flowers
>   In the heavy rain;
> But after beating showers
>   The sunbeams come again.
> Little birds are silent
>   All the dark night through;
> But when the morning dawneth,
>   Their songs are sweet and new.

--- *June 24.* ---

St. John Baptist.

A vessel unto honour, sanctified, and meet for the Master's use, and prepared unto every good work.—2 Timothy 2:21.

He must increase, but I must decrease.—John 3:30.

> Give us holy love and patience; grant us deep humility,
> That of self we may be emptied, and our hearts be full of Thee;
> Give us zeal and faith and fervour, make us winning, make us wise,
> Single-hearted, strong and fearless,—Thou hast called us, we will rise!

--- *June 25.* ---

O Lord, open Thou my lips; and my mouth shall shew forth Thy praise.—Psalm 51:15.

They shall shew forth My praise.—Isaiah 43:21.

How can the lip be dumb,
The hand all still and numb,
When Thee the heart doth see and own
Her Lord and God alone?
Tune for Thyself the music of my days,
And open Thou my lips that I may show Thy praise.

June 26.

THAT the name of our Lord Jesus Christ may be glorified in you, and ye in Him.—2 Thessalonians 1:12.

He traineth so,
That we may shine for Him in this dark world,
And bear His standard dauntlessly unfurled:
That we may show
His praise, by lives that mirror back His love,
His witnesses on earth, as He is ours above.

June 27.

THEN shall thy light break forth as the morning.—Isaiah 58:8.

Morning, morning on the mountains,
Golden-vestured, snowy-browed!
Morning light of clear resplendence,
Shining forth without a cloud;
Morning songs of jubilation,
Thrilling through the crystal air;
Morning joy upon all faces,
New and radiant, fresh and fair.

June 28.

THE Lord is my light and my salvation.—Psalm 27:1.
The Lord is my strength and song.—Psalm 118:14.

To-day the glowing sunlight
Is full and broad and strong;
The glory of the One Light
Must overflow in song;
Song that floweth ever,
Sweeter every day;
Song whose echoes never,
Never die away.

June 29.

St. Peter.

I HAVE loved you, saith the Lord.—Malachi 1:2.
Lovest thou Me? Follow thou Me.—John 21:17, 22.

Oh, let thy life be given,
Thy years for Him be spent;
World fetters all be riven,
And joy with suffering blent.
Bring thou thy worthless all:
Follow thy Saviour's call.

June 30.

Lo, I am with you alway, even unto the end of the world.
—Matthew 28:20.

He is with thee! yes, for ever!
Now, and through eternity.
Then, with Him for ever dwelling,
Thou shalt share His joy excelling,
Thou with Christ, and Christ with thee.

JULY.

———

Softly the dew in the evening descends,

    Cooling the sun-heated ground and the gale:

Flowerets all fainting it soothingly tends,

    Ere the consumings of mid-day prevail.

Sweet, gentle dewdrops, how mystic your fall;

Wisdom and mercy float down in you all.

Softer and sweeter by far is that Dew,

    Which from the Fountain of Comfort distils;

When the worn heart is created anew,

    And hallowèd pleasure its emptiness fills.

Lord, let Thy Spirit bedew my dry fleece;

Faith then shall triumph, and trouble shall cease.

W. H. H.

July 1.

FOR as the heavens are higher than the earth, so are My ways higher than your ways, and My thoughts than your thoughts.—Isaiah 55:9.

We can but wait for truth of tone,
For truth of modulation and expression,
With lowliest confession
Of utter powerlessness, content
To trust His thoughts and not our own,
Until the Maker of the instrument
Shall tune it in another sphere,
By His own perfect hand and ear.

July 2.

CLOUDS and darkness are round about Him: righteousness and judgment are the habitation of His throne.—Psalm 97:2.

There are clouds and darkness around God's ways,
And the noon of life grows hot;
And though His faithfulness standeth fast
As the mighty mountains, a shroud is cast
Over its glory, solemn and vast,
Veiling, but changing it not.

July 3.

FORGETTING those things which are behind, and reaching forth unto those things which are before.—Philippians 3:13.

Shall there not be
A summer yet for thee?
Without the checking frost of spring,
Without the eastern wind,
Without the fitful gleams that fling
A treacherous ray from rainbow wing—
These thou hast left behind!

July 4.

I WILL love them freely. From Me is thy fruit found.—Hosea 14:4, 8.

What though the rainbow fade away?
The light that gave it birth
Is still the same; and e'en the cloud
Hath blessed the parchèd earth.

What though the blossom fall and die?
The flower is not the root!
A summer sun may ripen yet
The Master's pleasant fruit.

July 5.

ARISE, shine; for thy light is come, and the glory of the Lord is risen upon thee.—Isaiah 60:1.

Arise and shine! The gold light
Fair morning makes for thee;
A tender and untold light,
Like music on the sea.
Light and music shining
In melodious glory,
A rare and radiant shining
On thy changing story.

July 6.

THAT, when His glory shall be revealed, ye may be glad also with exceeding joy.—1 Peter 4:13.

For light and life
End the war and crown the strife.
Joy to the faithful one full shall be given!
Rising in splendour that never shall set,
The morning of triumph shall dawn on thee yet,
When gladness and love for ever have met
In heaven.

July 7.

AND the angel . . . lifted up his hand to heaven, and sware by Him that liveth for ever and ever, ... that there should be time no longer.—Revelation 10:5, 6.

Then Time will seem but as a pebble cast
Into the ocean of eternity,
Breaking for one short moment the pure light
Which dwells upon its calm expanse of joy,
And in the depths of that translucent crystal
Bearing, deep-graven on its pale, clear front,
One word—REDEMPTION!

---------- *July 8.* ----------

THAT My joy might remain in you. That they may behold My glory.
—John 15:11; 17:24.

> O depth of holy bliss,
>   O depth of love Divine!
> What thought can measure this,—
>   *Thy* joy, *Thy* glory,—Thine!
> Yet this our treasure evermore;
> Thy fulness is Thy children's store.

---------- *July 9.* ----------

MY grace is sufficient for thee.—2 Corinthians 12:9.
And God is able to make all grace abound toward you.
—2 Corinthians 9:8.

> I am so needy, Lord! and yet I know
>   All fulness dwells in Thee;
> And hour by hour that never-failing treasure
> Supplies and fills, in overflowing measure,
> My least, my greatest need; and so
>   Thy grace is enough for me.

---------- *July 10.* ----------

BUT I am poor and needy; yet the Lord thinketh upon me.
—Psalm 40:17.

> O pity infinite!
>   O royal mercy free!
> O gentle climax of the depth and height
> Of God's most precious thoughts, most wonderful, most strange,
>   For I am poor and needy, yet
> The Lord, Jehovah, thinketh upon me!

---------- *July 11.* ----------

YOUR reasonable service.—Romans 12:1.

Take my life, and let it be
Consecrated, Lord, to Thee.
Take my moments and my days;
Let them flow in ceaseless praise.
Take my silver and my gold;
Not a mite would I withhold.
Take my heart; it *is* Thine own;
It shall be Thy royal throne.

July 12.

YE serve the Lord Christ.—Colossians 3:24.
Him only shalt thou serve.—Matthew 4:10.
I will not go away from Thee.—Deuteronomy 15:16.

I would not leave His service,
It is so sweet and blest;
And in the weariest moments
He gives the truest rest.
I would not halve my service,
His only it must be,
His *only*, who so loved me,
And gave Himself for me.

July 13.

VESSELS of mercy . . . prepared unto glory.—Romans 9:23.

Make us, in Thy royal palace,
Vessels worthy for the King;
From Thy fulness fill our chalice,
From Thy never-failing spring.

July 14.

ALL my springs are in Thee.—Psalm 87:7.

Thy love, Thy joy, Thy peace
Continuously impart
Unto my heart,
Fresh springs that never cease,
But still increase.

July 15.

THE Lord shall increase you more and more.—Psalm 115:14.
He giveth more grace.—James 4:6.

> Ever more and more bestowing,
> Love and joy in riper glowing,
> Faith increasing, graces growing,—
> Such His promises to you!
> He is faithful, He is true!

July 16.

THIS is the will of God.—1 Thessalonians 4:3.

> Blest will of God, whose splendour
> Is dawning on the world,
> On hearts in which Christ's banner
> Is manfully unfurled,
> On hearts of childlike meekness
> With dew of youth impearled.

July 17.

ELECT according to the foreknowledge of God the Father. Who are kept
by the power of God through faith unto salvation.—1 Peter 1:2, 5.

> Sovereign Lord and gracious Master,
> Thou didst freely choose Thine own,
> Thou hast called with mighty calling,
> Thou wilt save, and keep from falling;—
> Thine the glory, Thine alone!

July 18.

BUT we all, with open face beholding as in a glass the glory of the
Lord, are changed into the same image from glory to glory, even as
by the Spirit of the Lord.—2 Corinthians 3:18.

"From glory unto glory!" O marvels of the Word!
"With open face beholding the glory of the Lord,"
"We, even we (O wondrous grace!) are changed into the same,"
The image of our Saviour, to glorify His Name.

July 19.

WHO hath blessed us with all spiritual blessings in heavenly places in Christ: according as He hath chosen us in Him before the foundation of the world, that we should be holy.—Ephesians 1:3, 4.

Blessèd be the God and Father of our Saviour Jesus Christ,
Who hath blessed us with such blessings all uncounted and unpriced!
Let our high and holy calling, and our strong salvation be,
Theme of never-ending praises, God of sovereign grace, to Thee!

July 20.

THERE remaineth therefore a rest to the people of God.—Hebrews 4:9.

The glisten of the white robe,
The waving of the palm,
The ended sin and sorrow,
The sweet eternal calm,
The holy adoration
That perfect love shall bring,
And face to face, in glorious grace,
The beauty of the King.

July 21.

WHICH hope we have as an anchor of the soul, both sure and stedfast, and which entereth into that within the veil; whither the Forerunner is for us entered, even Jesus.—Hebrews 6:19, 20.

Anchorage within the veil,
Sure and stedfast, cannot fail,
Though the wildest storms assail.

— *July 22.* —

IN all their affliction He was afflicted.—Isaiah 63:9.

No sigh but from the harps above
Soft echoing tones shall win;
No heart-wound but the Lord of Love
Shall pour His comfort in.
They claim to rest on Jesu's breast
All weariness shall be,
And pain thy portal to His heart
Of boundless sympathy.

— *July 23.* —

THOU, Lord God, knowest Thy servant.—2 Samuel 7:20.

I could not do without Thee!
No other friend can read
The spirit's strange, deep longings,
Interpreting its need.
No human heart could enter
Each dim recess of mine,
And soothe and hush and calm it,
O blessèd Lord, but Thine.

— *July 24.* —

FOR I, saith the Lord, will be unto her a wall of fire round about.
—Zechariah 2:5.

They say there is a hollow, safe and still,
A point of coolness and repose,
Within the centre of a flame; where life might dwell,
Unharmed and unconsumed, as in a luminous shell,
Which the bright walls of fire enclose
In breachless splendour; barrier that no foes
Could pass at will.

— *July 25.* —

St. James

I HAVE led thee in right paths.—Proverbs 4:11.

At the portals of the Mansion, now he stands and gazes back.
There is light upon the river, light upon the forest track;
Light upon the darkest valley, light upon the sternest height;
Light upon the brake and bramble, everywhere that glorious light!

July 26.

I HAVE trusted also in the Lord.—Psalm 26:1.
I trust in Thee.—Psalm 25:2.
I will trust, and not be afraid.—Isaiah 12:2.

> Yes, I will trust, Lord Jesus!
> What Thou dost choose,
> The soul that really loves Thee
> Will not refuse.
> It is not for the first time
> I trust to-day!
> For Thee my heart hath never
> A trustless "Nay!"

July 27.

FAITHFUL is He that calleth you, who also will do it.
—1 Thessalonians 5:24.

Though we know there must be trials and there will be tears below,
Yet we know His glorious purpose, and His promises we know!
Only ask, "What saith the Master?" and believe His word alone,
That from glory unto glory He shall lead, shall change His own.

July 28.

ONE star differeth from another star in glory.—1 Corinthians 15:41.

> In those heavenly constellations,
> Lo! what differing glories meet;
> Stars of radiance, soft and tender,
> Stars of full and dazzling splendour,
> All in God's own light complete;
> Brightest they whose holy feet,
> Faithful to His service sweet,
> Nearest to their Master trod,
> Winning wandering souls to God.

————— *July 29.* —————

THE Lord shall be thine everlasting light, and the days of thy mourning shall be ended.—Isaiah 60:20.

> Where the blessèd harpers raise
> Alleluias evermore,
> And the billows of their praise
> Never die upon the shore;
> Where the eye grows never dim
> Gazing on that mighty Sun,
> Ever finding all in Him,
> Every joy complete in one.

————— *July 30.* —————

SHE communed with him of all that was in her heart.—1 Kings 10:2. We have found Him. Come and see.—John 1:45, 46.

> I came and communed with that mighty King,
> And told Him all my heart. I cannot say
> In mortal ear what communings were they.
> But would'st thou know, go too, and meekly bring
> All that is in thy heart, and thou shalt hear
> His voice of love and power, His answers sweet and clear.

————— *July 31.* —————

LOOKING unto (*Gr.* away into) Jesus.—Hebrews 12:2.

> Looking into Jesus,
> Wonderingly we trace
> Heights of power and glory,
> Depths of love and grace.
> Vistas far unfolding
> Ever stretch before,
> As we gaze, beholding
> Ever more and more.

AUGUST.

———

Our faithful God hath sent us
    A fruitful harvest-tide;
He summer boons hath lent us,
    And winter wants supplied.

The fields, at His ordaining,
    Stand thick with golden sheaves;
And man, full oft complaining,
    New bounty now receives.

Though Mercy largely giveth,
    Is Justice pacified?
We live through Him who liveth,
    The "Corn of Wheat" that died.

Then full be our thanksgiving,
    And clear each note of joy;
While faith and holy living
    Our earnest thoughts employ.

And, at the last Great Reaping,
    When Christ His sheaves will own,
May we, no longer weeping,
    Be garnered near His throne!

Praise we the Godhead Union,
    The Eternal Three-in-One:
With them may our communion
    For ever be begun.

W. H. H.

August 1.

THIS is the rest wherewith ye may cause the weary to rest; and this is
the refreshing.—Isaiah 28:12.

O rest so true, so sweet!
Would it were shared by all the weary world!
'Neath shadowing banner of His love unfurled,
We bend to kiss the Master's piercèd feet,
Then lean our love upon His loving breast,
And know God's rest.

August 2.

I SAT down under His shadow with great delight, and His fruit was
sweet to my taste. He brought me to the banqueting house, and His
banner over me was love.—Song of Solomon 2:3, 4.

Sit down beneath His shadow, and rest with great delight;
The faith that now beholds Him, is pledge of future sight.
His righteousness, "all glorious" thy festal robe shall be;
And love that passeth knowledge His banner over thee.

August 3.

SHINETH more and more unto the perfect day.—Proverbs 4:18.

How shall the light be clearer
    That is so bright to-day?
How shall the hope be dearer
    That pours such joyous ray?
I am only waiting
    For the answer golden;
What faith is ante-dating
    Shall not be withholden.

August 4.

Fruit unto life eternal.—John 4:36.

Gracious first-fruits here may meet thee of the reaping-time begun;
But upon the Hill of Zion, 'neath the uncreated Sun,
First the fulness of the blessing shall the faithful labourer see,
Gathering fruit to life eternal, harvest of eternity.

August 5.

Ye shall be gathered one by one.—Isaiah 27:12.
Yet shall not the least grain fall upon the earth.—Amos 9:9.

Of all His own He loseth none,
They shall be gathered one by one;
He garnereth the smallest grain,
His travail shall not be in vain.

August 6.

He shall see of the travail of His soul, and shall be satisfied.
—Isaiah 53:11.

Soon, soon our waiting eyes shall see
The Saviour's mighty Jubilee!
His harvest-joy is filling fast,
He shall be satisfied at last.

August 7.

No man can find out the work that God maketh from the beginning
to the end.—Ecclesiastes 3:11.
His work is perfect.—Deuteronomy 32:4.

For what we deem a symphony is but one thrilling bar,
Through the aisles of His great temple resounding full and far;
That which we deem an ocean is a shallow by the shore,—
For onward yet, and onward through the Infinite we soar.

August 8.

THE sea is His, and He made it.—Psalm 95:5.

The myriad-handed might
From which the million-teeming ocean fell,
No greater toil to Him,
From silent depth to surfy rim,
Than the small crystal drop which fills a rosy shell.

August 9.

AND now men see not the bright light which is in the clouds.
—Job 37:21.

The thunderous masses wildly drift
In lurid gloom and grandeur: then a swift
And dazzling ray bursts through a sudden rift;
The dark waves glitter as the storms subside,
And all is light and glory at the eventide.

August 10.

HE that doeth truth cometh to the light.—John 3:21.

So close to us, so very near,
Our inmost selves enfolding,
Discerning, penetrating;—we, beholding
Its terrible brightness, well might fear,
But for the glow
Of known and trusted love, that pulseth warm below.

August 11.

ENTER into His sanctuary, . . . and serve the Lord your God.
—2 Chronicles 30:8.
I will praise Thee with my whole heart.—Psalm 9:1.

Half-hearted! Saviour, shall aught be withholden,
Giving Thee part who hast given us all?
Blessings outpouring, and promises golden
Pledging, with never reserve or recall!

Half-hearted! Master, shall any who know Thee,
  Grudge Thee their lives, who hast laid down Thine own?
Nay! we would offer the hearts that we owe Thee,
  Live for Thy love and Thy glory alone.

August 12.

A ccepted in the Beloved.—Ephesians 1:6.
  Perfect in Christ Jesus.—Colossians 1:28.
Complete in Him.—Colossians 2:10.

  Accepted, Perfect, and Complete,
  For God's inheritance made meet!
  How true, how glorious, and how sweet!

  O blessèd Lord, is this for me?
  Then let my whole life henceforth be
  One Alleluia-song to Thee!

August 13.

G od hath from the beginning chosen you to salvation through
  sanctification of the Spirit . . . to the obtaining of the glory of
our Lord Jesus Christ.—2 Thessalonians 2:13, 14.

  Chosen—through the Holy Spirit, through the sanctifying grace
  Poured upon His precious vessels, meetened for the heavenly place;
  Chosen—to show forth His praises, to be holy in His sight;
  Chosen—unto grace and glory, chosen unto life and light.

August 14.

C all unto Me, and I will answer thee, and show thee great and
  mighty things, which thou knowest not.—Jeremiah 33:3.

  His wisdom and His glories passed before
    My wondering eyes in gradual revelation:
    The house that He had built, its strong foundation,
  Its living stones, and, brightening more and more,
    Fair glimpses of that palace far away,
  Where all His loyal ones shall dwell with Him for aye.

August 15.

THOU exceedest the fame that I heard.—2 Chronicles 9:6.
We have heard Him ourselves, and know that this is indeed the Christ.
—John 4:42.

> True the report that reached my far-off land
> Of all His wisdom and transcendent fame;
> Yet I believèd not, until I came,
> Bowed to the dust till raised by royal hand.
> The half was never told by mortal word;
> My King exceeded all the fame that I had heard.

August 16.

OF His fulness have all we received, and grace for grace. Believest
thou? thou shalt see greater things than these.—John 1:16, 50.

> Saviour, grace for grace outpouring,
> Show me ever greater things;
> Raise me higher, sunward soaring,
> Mounting as on eagle-wings!
> By the brightness of Thy face,
> Ever let me grow in grace.

August 17.

LOOK unto Me, and be ye saved.—Isaiah 45:22.
Him that is able to keep you from falling (*Gr.* stumbling).—Jude 24.

> Look away to Jesus,
> Look away from all!
> Then we need not stumble,
> Then we shall not fall.
> From each snare that lureth,
> Foe and phantom grim,
> Safety this ensureth,
> Look away to Him!

———— *August 18.* ————

I WILL lead them in paths that they have not known.—Isaiah 42:16.
He knoweth the way that I take.—Job 23:10.

> Not yet thou knowest how I bid
> Each passing hour entwine
> Its grief or joy, its hope or fear,
> In one great love-design;
> Nor how I lead thee through the night
> By many a varied way,
> Still upward to unclouded light,
> And onward to the Day.

———— *August 19.* ————

THEN we which are alive and remain shall be caught up together with them in the clouds, to meet the Lord in the air: and so shall we ever be with the Lord. Wherefore comfort one another with these words.
—1 Thessalonians 4:17, 18.

> O words of sparkling power, of comfort full and deep!
> Shall they not enter many a heart in a grand and gladsome sweep,
> And lift the lives to songs of joy that only droop and weep!

———— *August 20.* ————

HE shall see His face with joy.—Job 33:26.

> Now they see their gracious Master,
> See Him face to face!
> Now they know the great transition
> From the veiled to veilless vision,
> In that bright and blessèd place.

———— *August 21.* ————

THE Lord alone did lead him.—Deuteronomy 32:12.
With His glorious arm.—Isaiah 63:12.
To a city of habitation.—Psalm 107:7.

> Oh, lean upon His glorious strength!
> The way may not be long;
> And He will bring thee home at length
> To learn His own new song.

August 22.

WHO is this that cometh up from the wilderness, leaning upon her Beloved?—Song of Solomon 8:5.

> I could not do without Thee!
> I cannot stand alone:
> I have no strength or goodness,
> No wisdom of my own.
> But Thou, belovèd Saviour,
> Art all in all to me;
> And weakness will be power
> If leaning hard on Thee.

August 23.

AND Enoch walked with God . . . three hundred years.—Genesis 5:22.

> So may'st thou walk! from hour to hour
> Of every passing year,
> Keeping so very near
> To Him, whose power is love, whose love is power.
> So may'st thou walk, in His clear light,
> Leaning on Him alone,
> Thy life His very own,
> Until He takes thee up to walk with Him in white.

August 24.

St. Bartholomew.

THOU hast given a banner to them that fear Thee, that it may be displayed because of the truth.—Psalm 60:4.

Valiant for the truth.—Jeremiah 9:3.

> Unfurl the Christian Standard, and follow through the strife
> The noble army who have won the martyr's crown of life;
> Our ancestors could die for Truth, could brave the deadly glow;
> And shall we let the Standard fall, and yield it to the foe?

August 25.

IF they obey and serve Him, they shall spend their days in prosperity, and their years in pleasures.—Job 36:11.

For faith shall be the rosy crown on morn's unwrinkled brow,
The sparkling dewdrop on the grass, the blossom on the bough;
The gleam of pearly light within the snowy-bosomed shell,
An added power of loveliness in beauty's every spell.

August 26.

THAT we should bring forth fruit unto God.—Romans 7:4.

Let sunshine of Thy grace increase
The fruit of love, and joy, and peace;
With purple bloom of gentleness,
That most of all our home may bless;
While faith and goodness meet
In ruby ripeness, rich and sweet.
May these in me be found,
And ever to Thy praise abound.

August 27.

HAPPY are these thy servants, which stand continually before thee, and hear thy wisdom.—2 Chronicles 9:7.
O Lord, truly I am Thy servant.—Psalm 116:16.

Oh, happy are Thy servants, happy they
Who stand continually before Thy face,
Ready to do Thy will of wisest grace.
My King! is mine such blessedness to-day?
For I too hear Thy wisdom; line by line
Thy ever-brightening words in holy radiance shine.

August 28.

HIS servants shall serve Him.—Revelation 22:3.

"Shall serve Him" hour by hour,
For He will show me how!
My Master is fulfilling
His promise even now.
"Shall serve Him"—and for ever!
O hope most sure, most fair!
The perfect love outpouring
In perfect service there!

─────────── *August 29.* ───────────

Chosen . . . to give thanks to the Lord.—1 Chronicles 16:41.
O come, let us sing unto the Lord.—Psalm 95:1.
With my song will I praise Him.—Psalm 28:7.

Our harp-notes should be sweeter, our trumpet-tones more clear,
Our anthems ring so grandly, that all the world must hear!
Oh royal be our music, for who hath cause to sing
Like the chorus of redeemed ones, the Children of the King!

─────────── *August 30.* ───────────

God Himself is with us.—2 Chronicles 13:12.

"He is with thee! With thee always,
    All the nights and all the days;
Never failing, never frowning,
With His lovingkindness crowning,
    Tuning all thy life to praise.

─────────── *August 31.* ───────────

Thou hast the dew of Thy youth.—Psalm 110:3
I will be as the dew unto Israel.—Hosea 14:5.

Onward and upward still our way,
With the joy of progress from day to day;
Nearer and nearer every year
To the visions and hopes most true and dear;
Children still of a Father's love,
Children still of a home above!
    Thus we look back,
Without a sigh, o'er the lengthening track.

SEPTEMBER.

How calmly sinks the sun
   Beneath the western deep,
When day his giant course has run,
   And storm is hushed to sleep.

So like the sun would I,
   In tranquil eve descend,
And watch, with softly waning eye,
   The footsteps of the end.

But though, in darkness set,
   The sun seems lost awhile,
He will his shroud shake off, and yet
   Arise with joyous smile.

Thus, like the sun, may I
   Descend to rise again,
And meet my Saviour in the sky,
   With all His glorious train.

W. H. H.

September 1.

BEING filled with the fruits of righteousness, which are by Jesus Christ, unto the glory and praise of God.—Philippians 1:11.

> Press on, though summer waneth,
> And falter not, nor fear,
> For God can make the Autumn
> The glory of the year.

September 2.

HE hath done all things well.—Mark 7:37.

> This is praise,
> Deepest and truest, such as those may raise
> Who know both shade and sunlight, and whose life
> Hath learnt victorious strife,
> Of courage and of trust and hope still dear,
> With passion and with grief, with danger and with fear.

September 3.

I WILL bless thee, and make thy name great; and thou shalt be a blessing. —Genesis 12:2.

> Thy Spirit's fulness on him rest,
> Thy love his sunshine be;
> And may he still, while doubly blest,
> A blessing be from Thee.
> Be his the "everlasting name,"
> Inscribed by Thy own hand;
> That he the promised home may claim
> In Thine own Holy Land.

September 4.

THY will he done.—Matthew 6:10.
Understanding what the will of the Lord is.—Ephesians 5:17.

Blest Will of God! most glorious,
The very fount of grace,
Whence all the goodness floweth
That marvelling ages trace;
Temple whose pinnacles are Love,
And Faithfulness its base.

September 5.

THY will be done in earth, as it is in heaven. For Thine is . . . the power.—Matthew 6:10, 13.

Our Father, we pray that Thy will may be done,
For full acquiescence is heaven begun—
Both in us and by us Thy purpose be wrought,
In word and in action, in spirit and thought;
And Thou canst enable us thus to fulfil,
With holy rejoicing, Thy glorious will,
For Thine is the Power!

September 6.

MY people shall dwell . . . in quiet resting places.—Isaiah 32:18. He maketh me to lie down in green pastures: He leadeth me beside the still waters.—Psalm 23:2.

Resting in the pastures, and beneath the Rock,
Resting by the waters where He leads His flock,
Resting, while we listen, at His glorious feet,
Resting in His very arms! O rest complete.

September 7.

FOR he that is entered into his rest, he also hath ceased from his own works, as God did from His.—Hebrews 4:10.

Resting in the fortress, while the foe is nigh;
Resting in the life-boat, while the waves roll high;
Resting in the chariot, for the swift, glad race,
Resting, always resting, in His boundless grace.

September 8.

Go home to thy friends, and tell them how great things the Lord hath done for thee, and hath had compassion on thee.—Mark 5:19.

> Now I will turn to mine own land, and tell
> What I myself have seen and heard of Thee,
> And give Thine own sweet message, "Come and see!"
> And yet in heart and mind for ever dwell
> With Thee, my King of Peace, in loyal rest,
> Within the fair pavilion of Thy presence blest.

September 9.

The eternal purpose which He purposed in Christ Jesus our Lord.
—Ephesians 3:11.
God . . . sent Him to bless you.—Acts 3:26.

> O what everlasting blessings God outpoureth on His own!
> Ours by promise true and faithful, spoken from the eternal throne;
> Ours by His eternal purpose ere the universe had place;
> Ours by everlasting covenant, ours by free and royal grace.

September 10.

Having made known unto us the mystery of His will, according to His good pleasure which He hath purposed in Himself.—Ephesians 1:9.

> A splendour that illumines
>   Abysses of the Past,
> And marvels of the Future,
>   Sublime and bright and vast;
> While o'er our tiny Present
>   A flood of light is cast.

September 11.

Of His fulness have all we received.—John 1:16.

> The fulness of His blessing encompasseth our way;
> The fulness of His promises crowns every brightening day;

The fulness of His glory is beaming from above,
While more and more we realize the fulness of His love.

September 12.

THE Lord shall increase you more and more.—Psalm 115:14.
They shall increase as they have increased.—Zechariah 10:8.

Ever more and more bestowing,
Love and joy in riper glowing,
Faith increasing, graces growing—
Such His promises to you!
He is faithful, He is true!

September 13.

HE died for all, that they which live should not henceforth live unto
themselves, but unto Him which died for them, and rose again.
—2 Corinthians 5:15.

He is come to claim His throne,
And thy life is all His own.
Voices of this passing earth,
Echoes of its praise or mirth,
Reach not, when the heart hath heard
Golden music of His word.
"All for Jesus" henceforth be!
Live for Him who died for thee!

September 14.

O THAT thou hadst hearkened to My commandments! then had thy
peace been as a river.—Isaiah 48:18.
Great peace have they which love Thy law.—Psalm 119:165.

Like a river glorious is God's Perfect Peace,
Over all victorious in its bright increase.
Perfect—yet it floweth fuller every day;
Perfect—yet it groweth deeper all the way.

September 15.

THOU hast put off my sackcloth, and girded me with gladness; to the end that my glory may sing praise to Thee, and not be silent. —Psalm 30:11, 12.

> O the gladness of the spirit, when the True and Only Light
> Pours in radiant resplendence, making all things new and bright!
> When the love of Jesus shineth in its overcoming power,
> When the secret, sweet communion hallows every passing hour.

September 16.

Is not the Lord your God with you? and hath He not given you rest on every side?—1 Chronicles 22:18.

> Resting and believing, let us onward press,
> Resting on Himself, the Lord our Righteousness,
> Resting and rejoicing, let His saved ones sing,
> Resting in the mighty love of Christ our King.

September 17.

COME ye, and let us walk in the light of the Lord.—Isaiah 2:5. Consider how great things He hath done for you.—1 Samuel 12:24.

> O ye who seek the Saviour, look up in faith and love,
> Come up into the sunshine, so bright and warm above!
> No longer tread the valley, but clinging to His hand,
> Ascend the shining summits, and view the glorious land.

September 18.

WRITTEN not with ink, but with the Spirit of the living God. —2 Corinthians 3:3.

> Let Him write what He will upon our hearts
> With His unerring pen. They are His own,
> Hewn from the rock by His selecting grace,
> Prepared for His own glory. Let Him write!
> Be sure He will not cross out one sweet word
> But to inscribe a sweeter,—but to grave
> One that shall shine for ever to His praise.

September 19.

OUR gathering together unto Him.—2 Thessalonians 2:1.

All in perfect union brought,
Every link that God hath wrought
In the chain of loving thought;
All our dear ones, far asunder,
Each shall join the anthem-thunder
In our future joy and wonder.
All shall come where nought shall sever,
Endless meeting, parting never,
In God's house to dwell for ever.

September 20.

THE things which are not seen.—2 Corinthians 4:18.

Glimpses of glory, not far away,
Nearing and brightening day by day;
Golden crystal and emerald bow,
Lustre of pearl and sapphire glow,
Sparkling river and healing tree,
Everywhere palms of victory;
Harp, and crown, and raiment white,
Holy and beautiful dwellers in light;
A throne, and One thereon, whose Face
Is the glory of that glorious place.

September 21.

St. Matthew.

THAT the trial of your faith, being much more precious than of gold that perisheth, though it be tried with fire, might be found unto praise and honour and glory at the appearing of Jesus Christ: whom having not seen, ye love.—1 Peter 1:7, 8.

O words of holy radiance, that shine on every tear,
Till it becomes a rainbow, reflecting, bright, and clear,
Our Master's love and glory, so wonderful, so near!

September 22.

WHO is on the Lord's side?—Exodus 32:26.
Thine we are, David, and on thy side.—1 Chronicles 12:18.

> Teach us, Master, how to give
> All we have and are to Thee;
> Grant us, Saviour, while we live,
> Wholly, only, Thine to be.
> Henceforth be our calling high,
> Thee to serve and glorify;
> Ours no longer, but Thine own,
> Thine for ever, Thine alone.

September 23.

ALL that is within me, bless His holy name.—Psalm 103:1.

> I have no words to bring
> Worthy of Thee, my King,
> And yet one anthem in Thy praise
> I long, I long to raise;
> The heart is full, the eye entranced above,
> But words all melt away in silent awe and love.

September 24.

THIS is the victory that overcometh the world, even our faith.
—1 John 5:4.

> Increase our faith! On this broad shield
> "All" fiery darts be caught!
> We must be victors in the field
> Where Thou for us hast fought.
>
> Increase our faith, that we may claim
> Each starry promise sure,
> And always triumph in Thy name,
> And to the end endure.

September 25.

GOD that performeth all things for me.—Psalm 57:2.

Every joy or trial
Falleth from above,
Traced upon our dial
By the Sun of Love.
We may trust Him solely
All for us to do;
They who trust Him wholly
Find Him wholly true.

September 26.

WHERE the word of a king is, there is power.—Ecclesiastes 8:4.
I have put My words in thy mouth.—Jeremiah 1:9.
They shall withal be fitted in thy lips.—Proverbs 22:18.

I am trusting Thee for power,
Thine can never fail;
Words which Thou Thyself shalt give me,
Must prevail.

September 27.

HE that loveth Me shall be loved of My Father, and I will love him,
and will manifest Myself to him.—John 14:21.

The human heart asks love; but now I know
That my heart hath from Thee
All real, and full, and marvellous affection,
So near, so human! yet Divine perfection
Thrills gloriously the mighty glow!
Thy love is enough for me!

September 28.

IN His love and in His pity He redeemed them.—Isaiah 63:9.
How shall I give thee up?—Hosea 11:8.

Why should you do without Him?
It is not yet too late;
He has not closed the day of grace,
He has not shut the gate.
He calls you! hush! He calls you!
He would not have you go
Another step without Him,
Because He loves you so.

─────────── *September 29.* ───────────

St Michael and all Angels.

I WILL give him the morning star.—Revelation 2:28.

> See the singers before us in warrior chorus,
> Never despairing, and never yielding;
> Ever preparing and faithfully wielding
> Weapons kept bright and armour of light;
>   Shattering barriers that seemed adamantine,
> Spurning the depth and scaling the height.
> While, over all the turmoil and fray,
> Shines in the dawn that heralds the day,
>   Starlit, a crown amaranthine.

─────────── *September 30.* ───────────

THOU art worthy.—Revelation 5:9.

> "Worthy of all adoration
>   Is the Lamb that once was slain,"
> Cry, in raptured exultation,
> His redeemed from every nation;
>   Angel-myriads join the strain,
> Sounding from their sinless strings
> Glory to the King of kings;
> Harping with their harps of gold
> Praise that never can be told.

OCTOBER

"REST in the Lord!" Sweet word of truth—
A word for age, a word for youth;
A word for all the weary world—
A banner-word, by love unfurled.

Then cease, ye wearied ones of earth,
To slave for pleasure, gain, or mirth;
Cast down your load of vanities,
And welcome God's realities.

"Rest in the Lord!" Sweet word of grace
To all the Saviour's new-born race;
'Tis music, light, and balm to them—
An hourly guiding apothegm.[1]

Then, Lord of rest, we rest in Thee,
For all our daily destiny;
Our mighty guilt, our grief, our care,
We cast (strange act!) on Thee to bear.

For Thou, dear Lamb of God, wast slain,
To bear each load, and ease each pain:
And now Thy blood and righteousness
Are rocks of rest in all distress.

And when at last we fall on sleep,
Nor heart shall throb, nor eye shall weep;
Then, blessèd Saviour, let it be,
That Thou shalt write, "They rest in Me!"

W. H. H.

---

[1] apothegm: a short, instructive saying or maxim

October 1.

MIGHTY to save.—Isaiah 63:1.
Ready to save me.—Isaiah 38:20.

Reality in greatest need, Lord Jesus Christ, Thou art indeed!
Is the pilot real who alone can guide
The drifting ship through the midnight tide?
Is the life-boat real as it nears the wreck,
And the saved ones leap from the parting deck?
Is the haven real where the bark may flee
From the autumn gales of the wild North Sea?
Reality indeed art Thou, My Pilot, Life-boat, Haven now.

October 2.

LAY hold on eternal life, whereunto thou art also called.—1 Timothy 6:12.

A life is before thee which cannot decay,
A glimpse and an echo are given to-day
Of glory and music not far away.
Take the bliss that is offered thee,
And thou shalt be
Safe and blest for aye.

October 3.

AND Solomon told her all her questions: and there was nothing hid
from Solomon which he told her not.—2 Chronicles 9:2.

O happy end of every weary quest!
He told me all I needed, graciously,
Enough for guidance and for victory
O'er doubts and fears, enough for quiet rest;
And when some veiled response I could not read,
It was not hid from Him, this was enough indeed.

October 4.

THE Lord bless thee, and keep thee: the Lord make His face shine upon
thee, and be gracious unto thee: the Lord lift up His countenance
upon thee, and give thee peace.—Numbers 6:24–26.

The threefold blessing Israel heard three thousand years ago,
God grant it may on thee to-day in power and fulness flow!
For, faithful and unchangeable, each word of God is sure;
Though heaven and earth shall pass away, His promise shall endure.

October 5.

I CHANGE not.—Malachi 3:6.

All earthly love is as a thread of gold
Most fair, but what the touch of time may sever;
But His a cable sure, of strength untold—
  Oh, His love lasteth ever!
And this great love He will on thee bestow,
The fulness of His grace to thee make known,
Earnests of glory grant thee here below,
  If thou wilt be His own.

October 6.

EVEN every one that is called by My name: for I have created him for My glory.—Isaiah 43:7.

We are but little children,
  And earth a broken toy;
We do not know the treasures
  In our Father's home of joy.
Thanksgivings for creation
  We ignorantly raise;
We know not yet the thousandth part
  Of that for which we praise.

October 7.

THOU shalt make them drink of the river of Thy pleasures.—Psalm 36:8.

Infinite the ocean-joy
  Opening to His children's view;
Infinite their varied treasure,
Meted not by mortal measure,
Holy knowledge, holy pleasure,
Through Eternity's great leisure
  Like its praises, ever new.

—————————— *October 8.* ——————————

For with Thee is the fountain of life: in Thy light shall we see light.
—Psalm 36:9.

> By Him Life's Morning lovelit be,
> Who loved, and lived, and died for thee;
> So shall thy noontide never know
> Earth's burning thirst and withering glow;
> And thou shalt fear no gathering night,
> At Evening-time it shall be light.

—————————— *October 9.* ——————————

As thy days, so shall thy strength be.—Deuteronomy 33:25.

> As thy days thy strength shall be!
> This is quite enough for thee!
> He who knows thy frame will spare
> Burdens more than thou canst bear.
> When thy days on earth are past,
> Christ shall call thee home at last,
> His redeeming love to praise,
> Who hath strengthened all thy days.

—————————— *October 10.* ——————————

I shewed before Him my trouble. When my spirit was overwhelmed within me, then Thou knewest my path.—Psalm 142:2, 3.

> Father, I have said Amen,
> Said it often, now again.
> Father, strengthen it and seal;
> Let my weary spirit feel
> I am very near to Thee,
> For Thy hand is laid on me.

—————————— *October 11.* ——————————

It is the Lord: let Him do what seemeth Him good.—1 Samuel 3:18.

Thou wilt hear—I know not *how!*
Thou canst help, and only Thou;
So my prayer I leave with Thee.
Father, hear and answer me,
For the sake of Him who knows
All our love and all our woes.

October 12.

He for our profit.—Hebrews 12:10.
I am the Lord thy God which teacheth thee to profit.—Isaiah 48:17.

How sweet to know
The trials which we cannot comprehend
Have each their own divinely-purposed end!
He traineth so
For higher learning, ever onward reaching,
For fuller knowledge yet, and His own deeper teaching.

October 13.

Undertake for me.—Isaiah 38:14.
God that performeth all things for me.—Psalm 57:2.

No withered hope, while loving best
Thy Father's chosen way;
No anxious care, for He will bear
Thy burdens every day.

October 14.

There was silence, and I heard a Voice.—Job 4:16.

There are strange moments in the shadowy hours
Of slumber, when around the silent soul,
Touched by the influence of unseen powers,
Deep echoes of a spirit-music roll.
And those Eolian breathings seem to say,
Mortal, arise! thou art not *only* clay.

October 15.

Not knowing the things that shall befall me.—Acts 20:22.
He knoweth the way that I take.—Job 23:10.

'Tis a night of wonder at this call,
　　Characters cabalistic,
　　Writings all dim and mystic,
　　　Tremble upon the wall.
'Tis not mine to read them! Wait and see!
　　Wait for God's silent moulding,
　　Wait for His full unfolding,
　　　Wait for the days to be!

October 16.

Thou understandest my thought afar off.—Psalm 139:2.

For words are cold, dead things,
　　And little they tell of the heart,
Or the burning glow of the fount below
　　Whence the glance and the cheek-flush start.
Whose hidden depths within
　　Are ever "a fountain sealed;"
What the spirit itself has hardly seen
　　Is only to God revealed.

October 17.

Let thy garments be always white.—Ecclesiastes 9:8.
The blood of Jesus Christ His Son cleanseth us from all sin.—1 John 1:7.

What though by many a sinful fall
　　Thy robes have been defiled?
The Saviour's blood can cleanse them all,
　　And keep His trusting child.

October 18.

St. Luke.

THE Lord shewed him a tree, which when he had cast into the waters, the waters were made sweet.—Exodus 15:25.

The cure He hath devised, the blessèd Tree
The Lord hath shewn us, that, cast in, can heal
The fountain whence our bitter waters flow;
Divinest remedy,
Whose power we feel,
Whose grace we comprehend not, but we *know.*

October 19.

I KNOW whom I have believed, and am persuaded that He is able to keep that which I have committed unto Him.—2 Timothy 1:12.

Oh the freedom and the fervour after all the faithless days!
Oh the ever-new thanksgiving and the ever-flowing praise!
Shall we tempt the gaze from Jesus, and a doubting shadow cast,
Satan's own dark word suggesting, by the whisper " *If* it last"?

October 20.

BEHOLD, God is my salvation; I will trust, and not be afraid: for the Lord Jehovah is my strength and my song; He also is become my salvation.—Isaiah 12:2.

Lo! God is my salvation strong;
I trust, I will not be afraid!
Jehovah is my strength and song,
And my salvation He is made.

October 21.

I GAVE them My Sabbaths, to be a sign between Me and them.
—Ezekiel 20:12.

The token of His truth and care, the gift that He hath blessed;
The pledge of our inheritance, the earnest of His rest;
The diamond hours of holy light, the God-entrusted leisure!
Oh for a heart to prize aright this rich and heavenly treasure!

October 22.

A s the stars for ever and ever.—Daniel 12:3.

> Dear one, may thy life below
> Like a strain of music flow;
> Ever sweeter, purer, higher,
> Till it swell the angel-choir.
> Be thy life a star of light,
> Glistening through the dusky night;
> Till it shine with sunlike ray
> Through the One Eternal Day.

October 23.

M UCH more those members of the body, which seem to be more feeble, are necessary.—1 Corinthians 12:22.

> "What wouldst thou be?"
> A blessing to each one surrounding me;
> A chalice of dew to the weary heart,
> A sunbeam of joy bidding sorrow depart,
> To the storm-tossed vessel a beacon-light,
> A nightingale song in the darkest night,
> A beckoning hand to a far-off goal,
> An angel of love to each friendless soul.

October 24.

L ORD, all my desire is before Thee.—Psalm 38:9.
He will fulfil the desire of them that fear Him.—Psalm 145:19.

> Oh to be nearer Thee, my Saviour!
> Oh to abide in Thy dear favour;
> Oh to become each day more lowly;
> Oh to be made, as Thou art, holy;
> Oh to be ever upward gazing;
> Oh to be ever, ever praising;
> Oh to resound Thy love's sweet story;
> Oh to reflect Thy grace and glory!

October 25.

ABOVE all, taking the shield of faith, wherewith ye shall be able to quench all the fiery darts of the wicked.—Ephesians 6:16.

> Looking unto Jesus, never need we yield!
> Over all the armour, Faith the battle-shield!
> Standard of salvation, in our hearts unfurled!
> Let its elevation overcome the world.

October 26.

FEAR thou not; for I am with thee.—Isaiah 41:10.

> I am with thee! He hath said it,
>   In His truth and tender grace!
> Sealed the promise, grandly spoken,
> With how many a mighty token
>   Of His love and faithfulness!

October 27.

AND He said, My presence shall go with thee, and I will give thee rest. —Exodus 33:14.

> Through all the journey of *his* life, Thy presence with *him* go;
> Rest in Thee here, and with Thee there, do Thou, O Lord, bestow.
> Oh keep *him* faithful unto death; then grant to *him*, we pray,
> The crown of glory and of life that fadeth not away.

October 28.

St. Simon and St. Jude.

WHO crowneth thee with lovingkindness and tender mercies. —Psalm 103:4.

> Lovingkindness daily bright,
> Tender mercies every night,
> Be His crown upon Thy brow,
> Shining even here and now.
> Then the crown of golden light,
> Worn by those who walk in white,
> Won for thee by Him alone.
> Thou shalt cast before His throne.

---- *October 29.* ----

OTHER foundation can no man lay than that is laid, which is Jesus Christ. If any man's work abide which he hath built thereupon, he shall receive a reward.—1 Corinthians 3:11, 14.

> Glad surprise! for every service
> Overflowing their reward!
> No more sowing, no more weeping,
> Only grand and glorious reaping
> All the blessing of their Lord.

---- *October 30.* ----

WHAT I shall choose I wot not.—Philippians 1:22. My times are in Thy hand.—Psalm 31:15.

> Just when Thou wilt, Thy time is best,
> Thou shalt appoint my hour of rest,
> Marked by the Sun of Perfect Love,
> Shining unchangeably above.

---- *October 31.* ----

O MAGNIFY the Lord with me, and let us exalt His name together. —Psalm 34:3.

> All glory in the highest be to Him, our strength and song!
> May every heart uplift its part in blessing deep and long;
> Through Him who died that we might live, our glowing thanks ascend,
> The King of kings, and Lord of lords, our Saviour and our Friend.

NOVEMBER.

For ever and for ever, Lord,
    Thy kingdom shall endure;
Thy holy, lofty, sovereign word
    Its glory doth secure.

Bring on, bring on the promised day,
    Oh speed its eagle wing,
When earth, like heaven, shall Thee obey,
    And all the nations sing.

Grant us in firmest faith to stand,
    Full certain of the end;
And with Thy valiant little band
    Thine ancient truth defend.

O Jesu, be Thy cross our all,
    Thy crown our highest meed;
Nor saint nor angel will we call
    To help in time of need.

Thy Spirit give, and we will then
    Return Thee fervent praise;
And when Thou shalt come back again,
    A nobler song we'll raise!

W. H. H.

─────────── *November 1.* ───────────

All Saints Day.

ENTER thou into the joy of thy Lord.—Matthew 25:21.

> One by one, no longer gently bid to wait,
> One by one, they entered through the Golden Gate.
>   One by one, they fell adoring
>   At the Master's feet,
>   Heard His welcome, deep and thrilling,
>   "Enter thou!" each full heart filling,
>   All its need for ever stilling,
>   All its restless beat.

─────────── *November 2.* ───────────

EVERLASTING joy shall be upon their head.—Isaiah 51:11.

>   From the martyr and apostle
>   To the sainted baby boy,
>   Every consecrated chalice
>   In the King of glory's palace
>   Overflows with holy joy.
>   Sovereign choice of gift and dower,
>   Differing honour, differing power—
>   Yet are all alike in this,
>   Perfect love and perfect bliss.

─────────── *November 3.* ───────────

GOD hath from the beginning chosen you to salvation through sanctification of the Spirit and belief of the truth: whereunto He called you by our gospel, to the obtaining of the glory of our Lord Jesus Christ. —2 Thessalonians 2:13, 14.

> Then the gift, the free salvation, life in Him, through Him alone,
> Now in mighty consummation first in all its fulness known,—
>   Dower of glory all transcendent,
>   Everlasting and resplendent,
>   Is their own.

─────────── *November 4.* ───────────

THOU shalt forget thy misery, and remember it as waters that pass away.—Job 11:16.

Strong and joyous stands the traveller in the morning glory now,
Not a shade upon the brightness of the cool and peaceful brow;
Not a trace of weary faintness, not a touch of lingering pain,
Not a scar to wake the memory of the suffering hours again.

November 5.

THE Lord sitteth upon the flood; yea, the Lord sitteth King for ever.
—Psalm 29:10.

> Not yet thou knowest what I do
>   In this wild warring world,
> Whose prince doth yet triumphant view
>   Confusion's flag unfurled;
> Nor how each proud and daring thought
>   Is subject to My will,
> Each strong and secret purpose brought
>   My counsel to fulfil.

November 6.

IF children, then heirs; heirs of God, and joint-heirs with Christ.
—Romans 8:17.

> Heir thou art by His good pleasure,
>   All thy title Spirit-sealed!
> View thy grand and royal treasure,
> Every gift in Love's full measure,
>   Riches of His grace, so great,
>   Glory's far exceeding weight,—
> All in Christ for ever thine!
> Light, and Life, and Love Divine!

November 7.

FEAR not: for I have redeemed thee, I have called thee by thy name;
thou art Mine.—Isaiah 43:1.

> His own! But dare I say it, I,
> Who fail and wander, mourning oftentimes
> Some sin-made discord or some tuneless string?
> It would be greater daring to deny,
> To say "Not Thine," when Thou hast proved to me
> That I am Thine, by promise sealed with blood.

November 8.

AND he shall serve him for ever.—Exodus 21:6.

He chose me for His service,
And gave me power to choose
That blessèd, "perfect freedom,"
Which I shall never lose:
For He hath met my longing
With word of golden tone,
That I shall serve for ever
Himself, Himself alone.

November 9.

HE knoweth.—Psalm 103:14.

Yes, He knows the way is dreary,
Knows the weakness of our frame;
Knows that hand and heart are weary;
He in all points felt the same.
He is near to help and bless;
Be not weary; onward press!

November 10.

BE quiet; fear not.—Isaiah 7:4.

Thou layest Thy hand on the fluttering heart,
And sayest "Be still!"
The silence and shadow are only a part
Of Thy sweet will.
Thy Presence is with me, and where Thou art
I fear no ill.

November 11.

I HAVE covered thee in the shadow of Mine hand.—Isaiah 51:16.

Hidden in the hollow
Of His blessèd hand,

Never foe can follow,
Never traitor stand.
Not a surge of worry,
Not a shade of care,
Not a blast of hurry
Touch the spirit there.

November 12.

WHO teacheth like Him?—Job 36:22.
His way is perfect.—Psalm 18:30.

The ills we see,—
The mysteries of sorrow deep and long,
The dark enigmas of permitted wrong,—
Have all one key:
This strange, sad world is but our Father's school;
All chance and change His love shall grandly overrule.

November 13.

MY times are in Thy hand.—Psalm 31:15.
Your life is hid with Christ in God.—Colossians 3:3.

O strange mosaic! wondrously inlaid
Are all its depths of shade
With beauteous stones of promise, marbles fair
Of trust and calm, and, flashing brightly, there
The precious gems of praise are set, and shine
Resplendent with a light that almost seems divine.

November 14.

AND ye shall . . . be satisfied, and praise the name of the Lord your
God, that hath dealt wondrously with you.—Joel 2:26.

Yes, walk by faith and not by sight,
Fast clinging to My hand;
Content to feel My love and might,
Not yet to understand.
A little while thy course pursue,
Till grace to glory grow,
The what I am, and what I do,
Hereafter thou shalt know.

─────── *November 15.* ───────

THE throne of God and of the Lamb shall be in it; and His servants shall serve Him.—Revelation 22:3.

If sweet below
To minister to those whom God doth love,
What will it be to minister above?—
His praise to show
In some new strain amid the ransomed choir,
To touch their joy and love with note of living fire!

─────── *November 16.* ───────

THE Lord thy God turned the curse into a blessing unto thee, because the Lord thy God loved thee.—Deuteronomy 23:5.

No note of sorrow but shall melt
In sweetest chord unguessed;
No labour all too pressing felt,
But ends in quiet rest.
No conflict but the King's own hand
Shall end the glorious strife;
No death but leads thee to the land
Of everlasting life.

─────── *November 17.* ───────

EVEN so, Father: for so it seemed good in Thy sight.—Matthew 11:26.

And if it seemeth good to Thee, my Father,
Shall it seem aught but good to me?
Thy will be done! Thou knowest I would rather
Leave all with Thee.

─────── *November 18.* ───────

UNTIL the day break, and the shadows flee away.—Song of Solomon 2:17.

Just when Thou wilt, O Master, call!
Or at the noon or evening fall,
Or in the dark, or in the light,—
Just when Thou wilt! it must be right.

Just when Thou wilt, O Bridegroom, say,
"Rise up, My love, and come away!"
Open to me Thy golden gate
Just when Thou wilt,—or soon, or late.

November 19.

THAT the name of our Lord Jesus Christ may be glorified in you, and ye in Him, according to the grace of our God and the Lord Jesus Christ. —2 Thessalonians 1:12.

I would be my Saviour's loving child,
With a heart set free from its passions wild,
Rejoicing in Him and His own sweet ways,
An echo of heaven's unceasing praise!
A mirror here of His light and love,
And a polished gem in His crown above.

November 20.

IN whom also we have obtained an inheritance, being predestinated according to the purpose of Him who worketh all things after the counsel of His own will; that we should be to the praise of His glory. —Ephesians 1:11, 12.

Yea, let my whole life be
One anthem unto Thee,
And let the praise of lip and life
Outring all sin and strife.
O Jesus, Master! be Thy name supreme,
For heaven and earth the one, the grand, the eternal theme.

November 21.

WHOM I shall see for myself.—Job 19:27.

Is it for me, dear Saviour,
Thy glory and Thy rest?
For me, so weak and sinful,
O shall I thus be blessed?
Is it for me to see Thee
In all Thy glorious grace,
And gaze in endless rapture
On Thy belovèd Face!

November 22.

Sᴇᴛ your affection on things above, not on things on the earth.
—Colossians 3:2.

To see, and know, and love, and praise for ever,
The Son of God who died that we might live,
Where Sorrow, Sin, and Death can enter never,
And ever find new cause new songs of praise to give,—
O glorious prospect! How, how can we cling
To dim earth-dreamings, when such hopes are given?
Oh may we from this day, on faith-plumed wing,
No linger cling to earth, but soar in heart to heaven.

November 23.

O sᴇɴᴅ out Thy light and Thy truth: let them lead me; let them bring me unto Thy holy hill, and to Thy tabernacles.—Psalm 43:3.

Thy Light and Truth forth-sending
From Thy own radiant side,
Be Thou our Guard and Guide!
On Thee alone depending,
No darkness can affright!
Thy shield of Truth and Light,
Clear flashing through the night,
Is all-defending.

November 24.

Uɴᴛɪʟ the Lord come.—1 Corinthians 4:5.

Darkness and mystery a little while,
Then—light and glory,
And ministry 'mid saint and seraph band,
And service of high praise in the Eternal Land.

November 25.

Bᴇ thou faithful unto death, and I will give thee a crown of life. And His servants shall serve Him: and they shall see His face.—Revelation 2:10; 22:3, 4.

Look on to this,
Through all perplexities of grief and strife,
To this, thy true maturity of life,
Thy coming bliss;
That such high gift thy holy dower may be,
And for such service high thy God prepareth thee.

November 26.

THE earth shall be full of the knowledge of the Lord, as the waters cover the sea.—Isaiah 11:9.

For He must reign.—1 Corinthians 15:25.

Let Thy kingdom come, we pray Thee,
Let the world in Thee find rest;
Let all know Thee and obey Thee,
Loving, praising, blessing, blessed!

November 27.

I WILL come again.—John 14:3.

Thou art coming, O my Saviour!
Thou art coming, O my King!
In Thy beauty all-resplendent,
In Thy glory all-transcendent;
Well may we rejoice and sing!
Coming! In the opening east,
Herald brightness slowly swells;
Coming! O my glorious Priest,
Hear we not Thy golden bells?

November 28.

THE thing was true, but the time appointed was long.—Daniel 10:1.

Thou art coming! We are waiting
With a hope that cannot fail;
Asking not the day or hour,
Resting on Thy word of power,
Anchored safe within the veil.
Time appointed may be long,
But the vision must be sure:
Certainty shall make us strong,
Joyful patience can endure.

November 29.

Behold, thy King cometh unto thee.—Zechariah 9:9.

> Cometh in lowliness,
> Cometh in righteousness,
> Cometh in mercy all royal and free!
> Cometh with grace and might,
> Cometh with love and light,
> Cometh, belovèd, oh, cometh to thee!

November 30.

St. Andrew.

Leaving us an example, that ye should follow His steps.—1 Peter 2:21.
Who went about doing good.—Acts 10:38.

> Arise! To follow in His track, His lowly ones to cheer,
> And on an upward path look back with every brightening year.
> Arise! And on thy future way His blessing with thee be;
> His Presence be thy staff and stay, till thou His glory see.

DECEMBER.

THE FIRST ANNIVERSARY OF CHRISTMAS.

———

COME, shepherds, come, 'tis just a year
Since sweetest music woke our ear,
   And angels blessed our sight!
Come, lift your heart and tune your voice,
And bid the hills and vales rejoice,
   As on that glorious night.

'Tis just a year ago, we say,
When night shone out as clear as day,
   And heaven came down to earth.
How did we fear, how did we gaze,
Surrounded by the sudden blaze,
   And thrilled with sounds of mirth!

Come, shepherds, come, with prayer and song,
This night to be remembered long,
   Rejoice to celebrate!
With reedy pipe, chant forth who can
To God all glory, love to man,
   And peace in every gate!

'Tis just a year ago to-night,
From heaven came down the Prince of Light,
   Our guilty world to bless.
Let Gentiles now with Israel sing
Our Saviour, Brother, Friend, and King,
   Our promised Righteousness!

W. H. H.

December 1.

THIS same Jesus.—Acts 1:11.

He Himself, and not another,
   He for whom our heart-love yearneth,
Through long years of twilight waiting
   To His faithful ones returneth.
For this word, O Lord, we bless Thee,
   Bless our Master's changeless Name;
Yesterday, to-day, for ever,
   Jesus Christ is still The Same.

December 2.

A LITTLE while, and ye shall see Me.—John 16:16.

Thou art coming, Thou art coming!
   We shall meet Thee on Thy way;
We shall see Thee, we shall know Thee,
We shall bless Thee, we shall show Thee
   All our hearts could never say!
What an anthem that will be,
Ringing out our love to Thee,
Pouring out our rapture sweet
At Thine own all-glorious feet!

December 3.

TILL He come.—1 Corinthians 11:26.

A little while, though parted,
   Remember, wait, and love,
Until He comes in glory,
   Until we meet above.
Till in the Father's kingdom
   The heavenly feast is spread,
And we behold His beauty,
   Whose blood for us was shed!

December 4.

I HAVE given them Thy Word.—John 17:14.

He robed
In finite words the sparkles of His thought,
The starry fire englobed
In tiny spheres of language, shielding, softening thus
The living, burning glory. And He brought
Even to us
This strange celestial treasure, that no prayer
Had asked of Him, no ear had heard,
Nor heart of man conceived. He laid it there,
Even at our feet, and said it was His Word.

December 5.

I REJOICE at Thy word, as one that findeth great spoil.—Psalm 119:162.

All wonderingly from page to page we pass,
Owning the darkening yet revealing glass.
O mystery of tender grace!
We find
God's thoughts in human words enshrined,
God's very life and love with ours entwined.

December 6.

I TRUST in Thy word. I rejoice at Thy word.—Psalm 119:42, 162.

It is so sweet to trust Thy word alone;
I do not ask to see
The unveiling of Thy purpose, or the shining
Of future light on mysteries untwining;
Thy promise-roll is all my own,
Thy word is enough for me.

December 7.

AND the people rested themselves upon the words of Hezekiah king of Judah.—2 Chronicles 32:8.

Upon Thy word I rest,
So strong, so sure;
So full of comfort blest,
So sweet, so pure.
The word that changeth not, that faileth never;
My King! I rest upon Thy word for ever.

December 8.

THE writing which is written in the king's name, and sealed with the king's ring, may no man reverse.—Esther 8:8.

For He hath given us a changeless writing,
    Royal decrees that "light and gladness" bring;
Signed with His Name in glorious inditing,
    Sealed on our hearts with His own signet-ring.

December 9.

THY word was unto me the joy and rejoicing of mine heart.
—Jeremiah 15:16.

May its holy counsel, guiding,
    Lead thee on through joy or sadness;
Still abundantly providing
    Secret strength and hidden gladness.
Ever on thy pathway shining
    Living stars 'mid earthly night,
May its truth and grace entwining
    Gird thee with a robe of light.

December 10.

THOU hast given a banner to them that fear Thee, that it may be displayed because of the truth.—Psalm 60:4.

So, dauntlessly, will we unfurl
    Our banner bright and broad,
The cause of His dear Word of Life,
    Our cause, the Cause of God.

December 11.

THOU remainest. Thou art the same, and Thy years shall not fail.
—Hebrews 1:11, 12.

Reality, reality,
    Lord Jesus Christ, Thou art to me!
From the spectral mists and driving clouds,
From the shifting shadows and phantom crowds;

From unreal words and unreal lives,
Where truth with falsehood feebly strives;
From the passings away, the chance and change,
Flickerings, vanishings, swift and strange,
   I turn to my glorious rest on Thee,
    Who art the grand Reality.

December 12.

No night there.—Revelation 22:5.

O the love and light in that home to-night!
   O the songs of bliss and the harps of gold!
O the glory shed on the new-crowned head!
   O the telling of love that can ne'er be told.
O the welcome that waits at the shining gates,
   For those who are following far, yet near;
When all shall meet at His glorious feet
   In the light and love of His home so dear!

December 13.

And we beheld His glory, the glory as of the only begotten of the Father, full of grace and truth.—John 1:14.

O full of truth and grace,
Smile of Jehovah's face,
O tenderest heart of love untold!
Who may Thy praise unfold?
Thee, Saviour, Lord of lords, and King of kings,
Well may adoring seraphs hymn with veiling wings.

December 14.

Christ shall be magnified in my body, whether it be by life, or by death. For to me to live is Christ, and to die is gain.—Philippians 1:20, 21.

Just when Thou wilt! No choice for me!
Life is a gift to use for Thee,
Death is a hushed and glorious tryst
With Thee, my King, my Saviour Christ.

December 15.

IN Thy name shall they rejoice all the day.—Psalm 89:16.
My spirit hath rejoiced in God my Saviour.—Luke 1:47.

Thou art the sunshine of my mirth,
Thou art the heaven above my earth;
The spring of the love of all my heart,
And the fountain of my song Thou art;
For dearer than the dearest now,
And better than the best art Thou,
Belovèd Lord, in whom I see
Joy-giving, glad reality.

December 16.

HE performeth the thing that is appointed for me.—Job 23:14.

I am so glad! It is such rest to know
That Thou hast ordered and appointed all,
And wilt yet order and appoint my lot.
For though so much I cannot understand,
And would not choose, has been, and yet may be;
Thou choosest, Thou performest, THOU, my Lord.
This is enough for me.

December 17.

WE must through much tribulation enter into the kingdom of God.
—Acts 14:22.

Blessing is built upon this dark foundation;
And glorious temples rising from such woe,
Rising upon such mournful crypts below,
Are filled with light and joy and sounding adoration.

December 18.

THAT the trial of your faith, being much more precious than of gold that
perisheth, though it be tried with fire, might be found unto praise and
honour and glory at the appearing of Jesus Christ.—1 Peter 1:7.

Precious, more than gold that passeth, is the trial of your faith;
Fires of anguish or temptation shall not dim it, shall not scathe.
Your Refiner sitteth watching till His image shineth clear,
For His glory, praise, and honour, when the Saviour shall appear.

December 19.

COME, ye blessed of My Father.—Matthew 25:34.

Still shall the key-word ringing, echo the same sweet *Come*!
" Come " with the blessèd myriads safe in the Father's home;
" Come "—for the work is over, " Come "—for the feast is spread,
" Come "—for the crown of glory waits for the weary head.

December 20.

I AM glorified in them.—John 17:10.

Come nearer, Sun of Righteousness, that we,
   Whose swift, short hours of day so swiftly run,
So overflowed with love and light may be,
   So lost in glory of the nearing Sun,
That not our light, but Thine, the world may see,
   New praise to Thee through our poor lives be won.

December 21.

St. Thomas.

MY Lord and my God.—John 20:28.

There were strange soul-depths, restless, vast, and broad,
   Unfathomed as the sea;
An infinite craving for some infinite stilling;
But now thy perfect love is perfect filling!
Lord Jesus Christ, my Lord, my God,
   Thou, Thou art enough for me!

December 22.

THE Desire of all nations shall come.—Haggai 2:7.
With my soul have I desired Thee.—Isaiah 26:9.

Hush! while on silvery wing of holiest song
    Floats forth the old, dear story of our peace,
His coming, the Desire of ages long,
    To wear our chains and win our glad release.
Our wondering joy to hear such tidings blest
Is crowned with "Come to Me, and I will give you rest."

December 23.

THINE, O Lord, is the greatness, and the power, and the glory, and
the victory, and the majesty: . . . Thine is the kingdom, O Lord.
—1 Chronicles 29:11.

Let the sweet and joyful story of the Saviour's wondrous love,
Wake on earth a song of glory, like the angels' song above.
Father, haste the glorious hour! every heart be Thine alone!
For the kingdom, and the power, and the glory, are Thine own.

December 24.

THE good will of Him that dwelt in the bush.—Deuteronomy 33:16.

He came to bring a glorious gift,
"Good will to men!" and why?
Because He loved us, Jesus came
For us to live and die.
Then sweet and long the angels' song
Again we raise on high.

December 25.

Christmas Day.

SERVE the Lord with gladness: come before His presence with singing.
—Psalm 100:2.

"A Merrie Christmas" to you!
    For we serve the Lord with mirth,
And carol forth glad tidings
    Of our holy Saviour's birth.

So we keep the olden greeting,
With its meaning deep and true,
And wish "a merrie Christmas"
And a happy New Year to you.

December 26.

St. Stephen.

H E, being full of the Holy Ghost, looked up stedfastly into heaven, and saw the glory of God, and Jesus standing on the right hand of God.—Acts 7:55.

Looking up to Jesus
On the Emerald Throne,
Faith shall pierce the heavens
Where our Lord is gone.

December 27.

St. John.

W E know that we have passed from death unto life, because we love the brethren.—1 John 3:14.

The bright electric thrill
Of quick, instinctive union, more frequent and more sweet,
Shall swiftly pass from heart to heart in true and tender beat.
And closer yet, and closer the golden bonds shall be,
Enlinking all who love our Lord in pure sincerity;
And wider yet, and wider, shall the circling glory glow,
As more and more are taught of God that mighty love to know.

December 28.

Innocents' Day.

H E shall gather the lambs with His arm.—Isaiah 40:11.

If we could but hear them singing
As they are singing now,
If we could but see the radiance
Of the crown on each dear brow;
There would be no sigh to smother,
No hidden tear to flow,
As we listen in the starlight
To the bells across the snow.

December 29.

THE Lord hath done great things for us; whereof we are glad.
—Psalm 126:3.

Be glad and rejoice: for the Lord will do great things.—Joel 2:21.

"FROM GLORY UNTO GLORY!" What great things He hath done,
What wonders He hath shown us, what triumphs He hath won!
We marvel at the records of the blessings of the year!
But sweeter than the Christmas bells rings out His promise clear—
That "greater things," far greater, our longing eyes shall see!
We can but wait and wonder what "greater things" shall be!
But glorious fulfilments rejoicingly we claim,
While pleading in the power of the All-Prevailing Name.

December 30.

WHEN thou passest through the waters, I will be with thee; and
through the rivers, they shall not overflow thee.—Isaiah 43:2.

I could not do without Thee!
For years are fleeting fast,
And soon in solemn loneliness
The river must be passed.
But Thou wilt never leave me,
And though the waves roll high,
I know Thou wilt be with me,
And whisper, "It is I."

December 31.

SURELY I will be with thee.—Judges 6:16.

"Certainly I will be with thee!" Father, I have found it true:
To Thy faithfulness and mercy I would set my seal anew.
All the year Thy grace hath kept me, Thou my help indeed hast been,
Marvellous the lovingkindness every day and hour hath seen.

HOLY and Blessèd Redeemer, we pray Thee,
   Succour and help us in all time of need;
Trusting in Thee and Thy promise, oh, may we
   Always find solace, and always succeed.
Speak what Thou wilt, we will ever obey Thee;
   Honour and fear Thee in thought, word, and deed.

Thou art Almighty, All-wise, and All-gracious;
   Make us all humble, devoted, and true:
Clad in Thine armour, no foe will dare face us,
   Danger and trouble will cease to pursue.
Once let the soft arms of Mercy embrace us,
   Peace shall pervade us like sweet falling dew.

Blessèd and Holy Redeemer, we laud Thee,
   Source of all succour, help, comfort, and joy:
While in yon heaven bright angels applaud Thee,
   We with their echoes our tongues will employ.
None of Thy glory shall ever defraud Thee;
   All, in its fulness, Thy saints shall enjoy.

W. H. H.

[This poem by William Henry Havergal was the last piece in F.R.H.'s *Red Letter Days*.]

William Henry Havergal (1793–1870), pastor, scholar, musician, poet. He was an example of the believer as Paul wrote, "Be ye followers of me even as I also am of Christ." I Corinthians 11:1 F.R.H. was the youngest of his six children.

Printed in Great Britain
by Amazon

32713430R00073